FLIP CHARTS: How to Draw Them and How to Use Them

Library of Congress Catalogue Number 86-73086
ISBN 0-88390-031-9

Published by
University Associates, Inc.
8517 Production Avenue
San Diego, CA 92121-2280
(619) 578-5900

FLIP CHARTS

How to Draw Them and How to Use Them

Written and Illustrated by Richard C. Brandt

University Associates, Inc.

Contents

Chapter 1.

Introduction

This is not the great American novel. It'll never hit the *New York Times* Best Seller List. Furthermore, it is not intended as an academic tome loaded with theory and research. This is a handbook based on practical experience of things that work and things that don't work.

Early in my career as a full-time presenter/seminar leader, I had the good fortune to become a contract instructor for The Forum Corporation, located in Boston, Massachusetts. The occasion was the largest single training effort ever attempted. About sixty of us trained almost 18,000 Navy civilians (GS-13, 14, and 15) and certain Naval officers. The sessions were two-and-a-half days long, usually back-to-back. Each session was team-taught by a pair of contract instructors. The program was an outgrowth of the Civil Service Reform Act. It dealt with setting objectives and subsequent appraisal of perform-ance against those objectives. This was all accomplished in about eighteen months.

I conducted over forty of these sessions and rarely teamed with the same person twice. As a result, I worked with a number of talented and remarkable people. Most of what I know about making presentations and conducting adult semi-nars and workshops, I learned from The Forum and these people.

Many of my colleagues were quite proficient and had many years in front of adult groups. They used The Forum's pre-drawn charts as well as their own. I did the same. As we continued the contract and I did more programs, I became sensitive to my colleagues' flip charts, their content, and how they were used. People I considered outstanding presenters/ seminar leaders seemed to be unaware of the impact, or lack of impact, that their charts made on the participants. Some expressed difficulty and even frustration in dealing with, and working with, flip charts.

As a beginner, I was looking for every advantage to be a better presenter/seminar leader; flip charts appeared to be one of the areas where I had an edge. I heightened my sensi-tivity to the use and misuse of charts. I captured ideas I thought were good and made mental and written notes about difficulties I and my colleagues were having. Most of the time they were small difficulties in the use of color or positioning, but they did seem to make a difference.

I'm still trying to be the best presenter there is. So I'm always looking for those little things which will make a presentation or seminar more enriching and more meaningful. This small handbook assumes that most of my colleagues have the same goal. Since I've had numerous phone calls and questions about this publication, I think my assumption is correct.

Many of the items are things that some people have been doing for years; but then, some of us haven't been working with flip charts for years. This handbook helps reduce that experience gap. Some of the items may seem minor or inconsequential. I don't feel that way. As presenters and seminar leaders, we need effective tools to enhance understanding, the learning process, and the environment.

I believe even a few minutes of planning or thought can make a difference. Consider that one of the frustrations or difficulties presenters experience is whether or not the session or program they just completed actually was effective. Did it make any impact, any difference? Will someone *do* something?

Some time ago, I was asked by a large *Fortune 500* company to give my session on presentation techniques. The participants were recent college graduates in a management training program. In addition to the tutorials and demonstrations, each person made several presentations. One of the most rewarding moments of my career was when I received feedback from the management some months later. They indicated that this group of young people regularly made oral business presentations that were so much better than others of their company.

Expertise doesn't take a lot of additional time and effort, though it does take some. Expertise takes know-how. This handbook, perhaps, can make a good session a better one if the presenter uses some of the know-how expressed in it.

Let me address some concerns or qualifications. One dilemma I'll share is that I feel that any audio-visual aid is supplemental to the issue or learning point being raised. I always receive comments regarding the excellence of my flip charts and graphics. So much so, that I get concerned that the charts are dazzling the participants to the detriment of the content. My colleagues don't think so, but the thought comes up at times. Another comment that has been voiced, though not often, is that the graphics are condescending. Since I adhere to Chester Barnard's comment that the secret of failure is to try to please everyone, I've accepted that a very few people may be offended.

At times throughout the book, I make comments or judgments regarding the use of a particular tool, method, technique, or resource. These are subjective evaluations based on my style.

I don't advocate that every reader change his or her style to that of Rich Brandt's. But, I encourage you to try some of the ideas, perhaps adapt some of them. Part of the presenter's professionalism stems from feeling confident and comfortable in front of a group. If these confidence levels are significantly reduced by using some of the techniques mentioned on the following pages, then don't use them. But, remember that very few of us hit a home run the first time at bat. If you believe that presenting and training take skill, then some practice is required. Expand your style, enrich it . . . don't change it.

Throughout the book I will use the word "presenter" as a synonym for trainer, salesperson, instructor, facilitator, seminar discussion leader, or meeting leader, and a lot of others you can probably mention—anyone who has to get up in front of others and make a presentation. "Presenter" just makes life a lot easier. Similarly, the pronoun "his" refers to both genders, not as a sexist male orientation. My colleagues include many creative and proficient women from whom I've learned much.

The book is small. It says what has to be said, I hope, in as few words as possible. The words are mine. I've tried to write it as I'd say it. So, for better or worse, I accept responsibility. I've had fun with it and I hope you do too. If there's an area, point, or technique that I have missed and that could add to the usefulness of the book, please let me know. Write or call at the address or number below.

One final point and we'll get on with it. I wish to thank all the people who supplied ideas, material, and especially encouragement. If I tried to list them all by name I'd probably miss somebody. That would bother me a great deal. So, I hope that all of you who helped and who read this finished handbook will get some inner satisfaction, and that you can see a comment or illustration and say to yourself, *"That's my idea!"*

But even though I've just written that, I have to mention two people. One is my sister-in-law, Judy, who copy-edited the work a number of times, even though I had to chase her, by mail, all over Europe. She wrote me once that authors have often had a love/hate relationship with their editors. This one is all love. The other person is very special, my wife, Jan. She was the primary force behind the actual completion of the handbook. In addition, she typed, edited, ran to the printer, made valuable suggestions, as well as sandwiches, and kept hanging in there.

Richard C. Brandt
P.O. Box 29384
Richmond, Virginia 23229
(804) 747-0816

Chapter 2.

Basics

The use of visual aids in presenting or facilitating isn't new. Records indicate that they've been around for years. There are infinite examples and methods—whether the battle plan is drawn in the dirt with a stick or explained with a regiment of toy soldiers. One that I'm particularly fond of is the Hopi kachina doll. Although it is purchased and sought after by collectors for its beauty as an art form, it was originally used to teach young Hopi children various dances, ceremonies, and deities.

Though not the most sophisticated visual aid available in today's technology, flip charts are certainly the most used (perhaps also the most popular). This is probably because they are simple, inexpensive, versatile, and when used with thought and creativity, can be very effective.

I particularly like the simplicity of the flip chart. It can go anywhere. Furthermore, you're in control. You don't have to worry if the outlet is in the right place, if the bulb will burn out, darkening the room, and a lot of other things like that.

For example, my friend Gary Burdette told me of an impromptu flip chart session he had. While Gary was waiting to see a client, he prepared a flip chart presentation with a felt pen on a yellow legal pad. He hadn't intended to do that, but the session went marvelously.

Early research suggests that adults can learn through all of our senses, although some of us learn much better by *listening* to material, while others need *visual* stimulation. But this is only prioritized learning; all senses are involved. When we listen to a speaker, we also respond to his gestures, facial expression, posture, and inflection. When we attempt to pick up an object, this is not just a visual experience; we're also making some determination relative to its weight, mass, and other factors.

A recent experience at a pizza parlor in Virginia Beach brought this point home. My wife and I ordered a mushroom pizza. She ordered a soft drink and I ordered a beer. The waitress brought a massive frosted mug to the table. When I lifted it to take a swig, I splashed beer all over myself. What I perceived to be a heavy glass mug was, in reality, a light plastic one.

Consider that the average presenter speaks at a rate of about 125–145 words per minute. However, the audience's minds can accept information at four or five times that rate. It's no wonder that minds wander and that the receiver's mind wanders as the presenter speaks. The mind won't stay still. It wants to work, absorb, and otherwise be active. Flip charts can assist in picking up some of that excess capacity.

Flip charts are certainly versatile and can enhance many communication situations. However, they are not the answer to all presenting problems. I am continually re-evaluating my charts for ongoing programs. Most of the time it appears I'm cutting down on "predrawn" charts and substituting charts drawn "on-the-fly."

It is probably a good idea to define on-the-fly. It's a term I use to indicate a chart drawn as needed, or as a colleague termed it, "planned spontaneity." Recording participants' remarks (processing and/or publishing) during a discussion would be an example of a chart that is on-the-fly.

A key point to remember is that any audio-visual (AV) aid is selected after the objectives and content are resolved. At this point, the question is asked, *"What AV will enhance my ability to achieve the objective of my presentation?"* Too often, I see or hear people decide to make a slide presentation without any preparation or thought of what point they want to make or whether that is the appropriate audio-visual aid for this presentation. In one of the largest banks in the country, the mode of presentations is entirely overheads. As someone said, *"They have reduced the art of memo writing to the overhead projector."*

So, the advantage of flip charts is still relative to the presentation you want to make. *"Are flip charts the correct medium?"* is a question you still want to ask, even though flip charts are almost ubiquitous. Limited visibility is probably the flip chart's main drawback if the room or the audience is too large.

Some Uses for Flip Charts

To Inform

To inform is probably the primary function of charts, whether your goal is to describe the eight characteristics of good feedback or the virtues of a political candidate.

To Focus Attention

Our minds are constantly active. (Although I've had some participants who would cause me to question the universality of that statement.) We can capture that excess capacity to some extent through visual communication. Again, the multi-sensory approach I mentioned earlier increases learning and memory.

That focused attention to the chart has another big benefit. It permits the presenter to look at his notes. This eliminates the need (a common mistake) to read the chart itself. Duplicate the chart in your notes and you'll avoid this problem.

To Record

Recording (writing the comments on a flip chart in front of the group) can be used for focus and/or discussion. It gives the contributor a sense of ownership especially when they are his very words. The participant can say, *"I've been published."* I'll discuss recording later in the book but there are two points I'd like to make right now.

I was teaching a management seminar with a colleague. The participants had to read a short case and my colleague was leading a discussion around it. I watched my co-instructor recording particpants' comments. After posting three or four items and about to write another, the participant who offered the last observation said, *"Don't put down that management crap. Write what I said."*

My colleague was force-fitting the particpants' comments. He was paraphrasing and reshaping those comments to what he wanted. A rule to consider in this situation: condense but don't paraphrase! People like to see *their* words on the chart. They may not come right out and say it, but they'll be thinking it.

My second observation goes right along with the above. Any time you are recording or publishing participants' comments, try to avoid any value judgments. I'm talking about comments such as, *"That's very good."* There's no hard and fast rule here. But consider that if you don't say *"That's very good"* to Mary's contribution, after making a similar comment to Joe's, that Mary's may be interpreted as being a dumb remark. *"Thank you,"* covers a lot of ground in this situation.

Still, you want to encourage the group to participate. But encourage as a group. Some examples that you might use:

- *"Y'all did some nice work this morning."*
- *"Thank you for your active participation."*
- *"Obviously there's some experience in this group."*
- *"That's a good list."*

Instructions

Giving instructions appears to be a real trap for presenters. They know them so well, everybody knows 'em. Right? Wrong! Instructions for various exercises can be made more understandable through carefully structured charts and the thoughtful use of color. They can resolve potential confusion and even participant frustration.

I teach a program for The Forum Corporation called "Organization Climate Workshop." In the session, participants are asked to estimate and plot (on a graph) the required climate of their organizations along six dimensions. They are then given a feedback report showing the actual climate. The actual figures are also plotted on the same graph.

The workbook, in which the participants are posting the figures, is very detailed and explicit. Participants are asked to subtract the "actual" climate from the "required" climate. They are then asked to record the three dimensions with the highest "positive" result (gap) on another worksheet for subsequent analysis. That's when the fun begins.

Regardless of the amount of preparation, of walking them through an example, and of explanation, at least a few participants have a great deal of difficulty with this simple exercise. Simple to me—I've seen it dozens of times.

One difficulty has been the word "positive." Positive can mean mathematically positive, a plus answer. Many think that positive means good. It obviously doesn't in this case. But even without that confusion they aren't on top of the instructions the way I know they could be. Only when I start using charts, particularly plotting the two sets of figures, do we overcome the problems I've mentioned with this exercise.

At the top of the next page are two charts that I would typically use in any round robin role play. A round robin role play is a training exercise designed to give people practice in a particular skill or technique. In small groups (usually of three) participants switch roles through successive rounds so that each has an opportunity to participate in a different role. In our example, the three roles include a manager, a subordinate, and an observer. I uncover the charts one at a time and test

ROUNDS	RD. 1	RD. 2	RD. 3
	40 MIN.	40 MIN.	40 MIN.
A	SUBORD. 17-18	MGR. 26-27	OBS. 14-15
B	OBS. 14-15	SUBORD. 23-24	MGR. 32-33
C	MGR. 20-21	OBS. 14-15	SUBORD. 29-30

ASSIGNMENTS	TRIO 1	TRIO 2	TRIO 3	TRIO 4	TRIO 5
	TOM	TIM	TESS	TOD	TERRY
	SUE	SAM	SALLY	SHARI	SILAS
	BOB	BETTY	BILL	BABS	BUBBA

for understanding as I uncover them. Notice that use of color adds to the clarity around the shift of roles. The charts wouldn't be nearly as effective without color.

Enhance the Learning Process

Someone once said we retain:

- 25% of what we hear.
- 45% of what we see.
- 65% of what we see and hear.

Some might argue with the accuracy of the percentages, but the fact remains that visual aids (in our case flip charts) do increase retention, by involving more of the mind's excess capacity.

Look at the chart at the right. I could just talk my way through the subject matter but that wouldn't be as effective as drawing the chart on-the-fly in concert with the comments being made. What's a bit unusual with this presentation is I begin at the bottom by saying, *We're all looking for the bottom line, call it performance."* I then build up to the three factors that impact organizational climate—internal, external, and management practices. Management practices, the things a manager does or doesn't do, account for more than 70% of the influence on the climate.

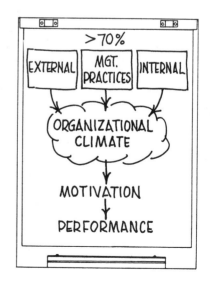

Even small groups can benefit from graphically portraying the comments made. Visuals permit new insights and a better, perhaps broader, perspective.

Discussion Structure

Of the four basic teaching modes (setting the climate, presentations, giving instructions, and leading discussions), leading discussions is the most difficult for me. Perhaps it's because I have the least amount of control in this setting. In addition, I'm always worried if the discussion will go where I want it to. I know that last point is wrong, after all, it's their discussion, but still . . .

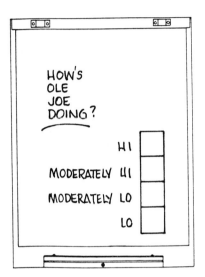

Charts can really help here in a variety of ways. One example is using a vote at the end of reading a case. Instead of just asking, *"How many of you think Joe is doing a good job?"* use a chart such as the one at the left. Note that an even number of options is provided. This requires the participants to take a stand, they can't sit on the "average" fence that might exist if there were an odd number of options. What you want to do is polarize the audience's view of the situation. At this point, the *"Why do you feel that way?"* questions can take over.

Listing pros and cons can also start the ball rolling. A key here is not to be judgmental about whether an item is a pro or con (plus or minus) until after you've written it down. If no one else challenges a wrong, or questionable categorization, you might ask for examples of that behavior to clarify understanding.

Another question might be, *"Do you all agree with that?"* Ideally, you would hope that someone would challenge it as soon as you finish writing.

If the challenge comes to you, it is time for a redirect. This might take the form of, *"Don't tell me, tell Harry, he's the one who said it."*

Brainstorming Sessions

Brainstorming is a popular technique but one which most people only think they know. I'm not going to go into the correct methodology for brainstorming in this little book; however, one of the important procedures is to write down (where everyone participating can see) *all* the items or alternatives being offered. The only feasible way to do this is with a flip chart, preferably two of them.

Printing where everyone can see the items helps people to build on each other's ideas and spurs new options that might not have been considered.

Display

I did a presentation session for a large corporation where the standard presentation medium was overheads. The culture, the top executives, demanded them—very much like the bank that I mentioned earlier. Incidently, they were very poor overheads at that. They had no color, except those that were done entirely in red. Try all red sometime, it's very hard to see. In addition, they were crowded; they had too much on them. This was probably a result of being too easy to make. Most were typewritten and difficult to read because of the size of the print.

When I tried to get them to consider flip charts, it was as if I was advocating anarchy, free love, and nationalization of all *Fortune* 500 companies! Every attempt at logical reasons for why they should at least try flip charts was met with utter disdain. Finally one of these proper conservative executives said to me, *"Rich, anything you can do with a flip chart we can do with an overhead!"* I thought about that for two seconds and replied, *"I can hang my charts on the wall."*

Let me explain. When I finish a session the walls will be covered with charts. I attach them, very carefully, with drafting or masking tape. I say carefully because if it is one of my predrawn charts that I'll use again, I don't want it torn. I attach my charts to the pad with transparent tape. In order to remove the chart from the pad, I cut it off with my pocket knife. The knife is one of the tools we'll discuss in the next chapter. When I put a chart on the wall, the masking tape only touches the chart where the transparent tape is. This prevents a lot of tearing and damage to the chart itself.

The types of charts you might consider hanging on the wall are: the overall objects of the session; participants expectations, reservations, and perceived obstacles expressed during the introduction; the schedule; key models or processes; key thoughts that you want to hammer home, build on, or refer back to later; and key learning or summary points. Charts that I would not hang on the wall include agendas, exercise instructions and assignments, and short term processing charts.

Let me provide you with some tips on hanging your charts on the wall. Presenters usually encounter two difficulties in this exercise. The first is getting them high enough, while the second is having them aligned, laterally even.

Let's discuss height first. The secret is not to try and hang them from the ceiling. Your audience is probably sitting down. That means that if the top of the chart is around seven feet from the floor, everyone will see it. So, don't stand on a chair

or even on your toes. Put your tape on the chart first and then, standing flat-footed, affix the chart to the wall. Doing this eases the second problem.

Having your charts all in line, vertically and horizontally, takes a bit more effort, but only a bit. If you've done what I said above, the chances are good that they'll all be at relatively the same height. A difference of a half inch or so isn't going to be objectionable. The key is to hang them perpendicular to the floor. How to do that? One way is to look at the texture of the wall. Is there a vertical pattern or seam that you can key on? If you've done a good job on the first chart (by inspection) key off that one for the next one. If you want a little more precision, use your yard stick as a plumb line. By holding it loosely at one end between two fingers, at arm's length, you can judge the vertical alignment of your chart.

Presenters/facilitators at a bank in California use an efficient technique for hanging charts on the wall. They put two small strips of transparent tape at the top of the page that will hold their predrawn chart on the pad. A piece of masking tape is then doubled over on itself and attached to each strip of transparent tape. The predrawn chart is then attached to the masking tape. When they want to hang the chart on the wall they remove the chart and the masking tape at the same time. That same tape is then used to attach the chart to the wall. You can't see the tape and it's fast. This technique is particularly effective when you want to display a chart immediately after talking about it. If your planning is good, the same technique can be used with a chart drawn on-the-fly.

I don't put them all up there but I do display quite a few. I think there's a tremendous advantage to being able to go back and relate a current point with a previous one; to remind people of where we've been, and so on. But, pay attention to the type of wall you're working with. After all, you want to be invited back. Drafting tape seems to do less damage than masking tape but I don't think it's as sticky.

I can recall coming back to an organization about three months after a session to do another one. We'd been working in the board room. The walls were covered with little spots where the paint had come off when they pulled off the masking tape. Since that experience, I always ask about painted walls. It's not a problem with fabric-covered walls, only certain painted ones. If no one knows what will happen, I test the wall in a low, inconspicuous spot. I suggest you do the same.

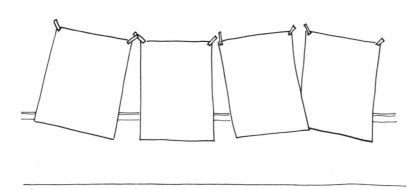

I did a session at a big hotel and asked about the walls. Everything was all right. That evening after the first day, I hung charts on the wall and set up the charts for the next day. When I arrived the next morning, all the charts that were on the wall, as well as the easels, were gone. The room had been sold for an evening banquet. I finally found the easels, but all the charts on the wall had been thrown away. So, another question to ask, especially with hotels, *"Has the room been sold tonight?"*

There are substitutes for tape, some that I'm sure you've used at one time or another, such as stick pins, straight pins, magnets, and clips. One that is simply marvelous is a small plastic clip that has a soft wax-like stickum on the back. The stickum adheres to just about any surface and seems to stick forever. In addition, the clips are reusable. Since the chart slips under the small pressure clip, it is less apt to become frayed or damaged.

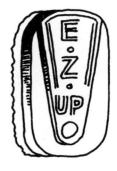

I received a few of these simple clips from Ray Cienek when I did a seminar for his company, Human Dynamics. One source for this tape is Stikky Wax Corp. in Chicago, IL 60612 (stock # 220).

The drawing at right is twice actual size. The printing is molded into the white plastic and very faint. Unless you're looking for it you may never notice the letters.

In the next few pages of this unit we'll look at common problems people have with flip charts.

Problems Using Flip Charts

Time

Not enough time to prepare is a common problem that generally heads the list of most presenters. First off, let me say that the time required to make a session the best it can possibly be is not a luxury. Neither is it to be viewed as a distasteful activity. That time is the effort the pro knows is necessary for a top-notch job. To some of you that probably sounds corny. My papa always said that *"good enough is no damned good."* But that probably doesn't apply to anyone reading this book. You're reading it in order to do a better job on your next presentation.

There are ways to reduce the time required. Some examples are: predrawn charts (carry them from session to session); convert predrawn charts (selectively) to on-the-fly ones; lay your charts out in your notes so you don't have to plan them each time out; and finally, practice.

The rest of the problems will be discussed in various sections of the handbook. These are:

Spelling

This is a problem I have all the time. This book can't make you a better speller but I have some hints on things to do.

Finding the Right Chart

Finding the chart you're looking for seems to be a difficulty a lot of presenters have experienced on occasion. There are some who flat out won't use more than one easel for that reason. Did you ever see someone lose a chart with only one easel? It's hard to do but I've seen it happen! I'll provide five pointers in this area that should help.

Printing

All you non-draftsmen are always concerned with your printing. Well, I guess that's not entirely true. I know there are some presenters who don't give a hoot. Hand printing will be discussed in some detail in Chapter 4, Design and Technique. However, the suggestions only help if you practice, and I don't mean during your next presentation.

The other part of this problem is *"I can't print fast enough to keep up with the audience!"* I'll discuss this later on when I address printing in detail, but this problem is usually coupled with the dilemma of having too much data and not taking enough time. That sounds like a paradox but it really isn't. One key solution is to not write too much. The chart is not a steno pad; it is used to focus on the key items, the key thought or concept. Where you stand in relation to the easel also affects your writing speed.

Charts Wear Out, Get Beat Up

This is a problem in handling, storage, and transportation. One reason I don't like people to use my charts is that most of them don't know how to take care of them. The result is that they do get beat up. This isn't a matter of their being careless; they just don't know how to properly handle flip charts. A number of ideas for care are offered.

Presenter is Short

This last problem is one that this little book can't do much about: being too small to easily turn the pages. You can shorten the legs of the easel—just remove the rubber plug and cut three or four inches off each leg with a hack saw. However, there really isn't a great deal to suggest.

With all the problems, flip charts are great tools in the learning environment. The problems and disadvantages are well offset by the many advantages and uses. The net of it all is that flip charts are more than just a big piece of paper. They are dynamic and effective when presented with know-how and thought.

Chapter 3.

The Tools

Some time ago, I did a program at Eagle Lodge in Lafayette Hills when the conference center had only been opened a few months. Eagle Lodge is located just outside of Philadelphia. I haven't worked all the conference centers in the United States, but I can't imagine a finer one. I've been back numerous times and it's always a pleasure to work there.

During that first session I had the good fortune to meet the man involved with construction and various contracts. He told me that as the lodge neared completion, they sent out RFP's (Request For Proposals) to a number of companies to actually manage the conference center. His comments were very interesting. The RFP went out to large hotel chains and management organizations. He said, *"They may know how to run a hotel but they don't know anything about running a conference center."*

Unfortunately, I knew exactly what he was talking about. I can arrive at a luxurious hotel, find a great room, plenty of space, well lighted, and then become concerned. Why? Instead of nice sturdy flip chart stands, I find tripods. Tripods with three thin legs held together at the top with flimsy hinges—the kind that you're reluctant to write on 'cause they'll fall down.

Like any skilled craftsman, or, as my papa would say, *"Ein Meister,"* the more you know about your tools, the more proficient you'll become. I've always noticed that as a result of my attention to (or is it preoccupation with?) flip charts, the more picky I've become.

This chapter of the book deals with the flip chart as a physical tool. It's not as exotic as something out of *Brookstone's* catalog, but to a trainer it's a specific and essential tool.

The Easel

I've already pointed out that not all easels are built and designed equally. There are probably two dozen or more easels available on the market. We've all been exposed to a variety.

However, the A502 introduced by Oravisual (now a part of Da-Lite Screen Company) in 1946 is hard to beat. You can buy more expensive easels, with fancy gimmicks you'll never use,

but the A502 is a value. At this writing, its price is about 160 dollars. It's simple, sturdy, and relatively portable. I purchased three when I started my business and they still look like new.

If you can't insist on and get an Oravisual A502, try at least for these characteristics in the easels you'll be working with:

- The easel should have a back plate that extends over the entire pad. It is extremely difficult to write on a pad without backing, especially the bottom third near the corners.

- The legs should be braced for stability. If that isn't possible, a chain or string should be tied to the legs restricting how far apart they can be spread. By standardizing the spread of the legs, all pads (and thus charts) will have the same tilt or lean.

- The above refers to all easels at the same angle; they should all be the same height. It's disturbing to have three predrawn charts that do not line up horizontally.

- A tray, attached to the easel below the pad, is nice but hardly essential. Few easels that had a removable tray when purchased still do.

- The easel should be capable of holding at least one full pad of paper (fifty or sixty sheets) and preferably two pads. If you put two pads on the easels, be sure to tear (cut) off the cardboard backing on the top pad before you place it on the easel.

- Finally, avoid easels that clamp the pads in place. It is almost impossible for one person to mount a pad in a clamp with the easel standing up . . . at least it is for me!

The Pad

Let's turn our attention to the paper pads themselves. The standard size is 27 inches wide and 34 inches long, but you will find some variations. They come in about a half dozen weights, textures, and thicknesses. Our discussion throughout will concentrate on the use of the large pads. Even so, there are a variety of formal and informal flip charts which can be used effectively in specific situations.

Recall my earlier comment about Gary Burdette using a yellow legal pad. A stenographic pad is well suited for a one-on-one presentation.

Most steno pads have a gummy edge at the bottom so that they'll stand without slipping. The stiff cover, designed for lap-writing, provides stability. The wide space between lines and split page are excellent for positioning your content. If you decide to use this tool, I suggest you test the size of your printing. Using the broad edge of an El Marko™ marker will probably be too wide. The small point (tip) of the El Marko™ or a felt pen will usually be fine. Remember that your audience will only be across the desk, perhaps four to six feet away.

There are other more formal easels available in different sizes and varying prices. I'm sure that most of you have seen the three-ring binder whose bottom fans out so that the binder stands up. We use a very nice small easel/binder by Joshua Meier Division of W. R. Grace & Company. The sheets are 11 × 14 inches and are great for sales, one-on-one, or other small audiences.

But let's get back to our standard flip chart pads and the paper on them. The least desirable is newsprint. Conference centers and clients usually don't offer newsprint. Hotels, however, will frequently offer it. It is terrible. It's grey and flimsy, it bleeds, and it's brittle. It should never be used for any chart that will be used more than once.

At the other end are some heavy papers, almost card or tag stock, and plastic-based paper. The latter is tear-resistant, resists curling, can be rolled and unrolled, and is very expensive. Twelve sheets of this plastic-based paper cost about twenty-six dollars.

The standard paper weight varies, depending on the manufacturer; but it's usually around sixteen pounds. In the past, I've used 16-pound paper almost exclusively. The only time I didn't is when the client or conference center had something different. For the last year or so I've been using 26-pound vellum for my predrawn charts and 16-pound for those of the planned spontaneity variety. I find that charts drawn on the heavier paper seem to hold up longer. The disadvantages are that the heavier paper is twice as expensive as the lighter one; and because of its thicker sheets, my chart carrier gets filled up faster.

A characteristic that is very important is whether or not the paper has a light blue grid. As I carry my predrawn charts from program to program, I'm not surprised when participants in the various sessions marvel at the light blue grid. But I am surprised when trainers, in my Presentation Skills or Train-the-Trainers programs, haven't heard of pads with a light blue grid.

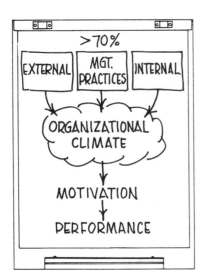

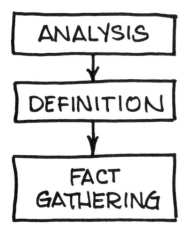

For some reason, Oravisual just discontinued their 27 × 34-inch 16-pound paper with a one-inch light blue grid. If you want a one-inch grid, you have to use 24 × 34-inch paper. If you want 27 × 34-inch paper, you have to use a half-inch grid. The latter is a bit more difficult to work with since most of the printing and spacing on such a large chart is in one- or two-inch increments. There still are manufacturers of one-inch 27 × 34-inch pads.

The light blue grid is the crutch for those of us who can't write or print on a straight plane, or can't keep our bullets lined up as they should be, one on top of the other. There are other advantages:

- It permits the presenter to print in a straight horizontal plane. We'll talk more about this in the next Chapter, Design and Technique.

- It allows you to line up margins, subheadings, and bullets.

- It permits a sense of symmetry and spacing to be injected into a particular chart. This is especially true for charts drawn on-the-fly. Naturally, you can do the same thing with a blank page, but it sure is easier with the grid.

Look at the "cloud" chart at the left. It's the same one as on page 9. I've drawn that chart so many times I can see it in my sleep. But I draw light pencil lines on the chart every time so that the boxes and printing are symmetrical. I think it's important and makes a difference.

While we're mentioning boxes, let me add a brief comment on drawing boxes with words in them. Very often, presenters draw the box and then find they can't get all of the word, or words, in the box they've drawn. This usually can be corrected by printing the words first and then drawing the box around the words. For symmetry and appearance, try drawing all the boxes the same width but extend the depth if more words are required.

The difference in cost between the plain paper and the grid paper is one dollar per pad or two cents per sheet. I believe it's well worth it. I don't agree with the comment made in a training magazine a year or so ago that working with ruled paper is for amateurs. We don't criticize a plumber when he comes to fix the pipes with a specialized tool.

But, each of you will probably work at some time with chart pads that don't have that marvelous light blue grid. So, what to do about it? The biggest problem with these blank pages is not the predrawn chart but the one drawn on-the-fly. The difficulties are writing on a straight line and overall spacing. That's why the grid is so important. There are a couple of solutions, but only one that I think is really feasible. That answer is to get a yard stick and lightly draw penciled lines two inches apart.

The argument always offered is that drawing all those lines takes time. My reply is yes, it does take some time, perhaps three to four minutes to draw ten lines on a page. The question you have to ask yourself: is it worth the three to four minutes to do a more professional job?

Predrawn chart spacing can be accomplished by filling an entire page with lines spaced two inches apart. Use a permanent black marker, and place this page under the one you're working on so you can see the lines through the paper. In effect you have a "cheater bleeder" page.

One thing we haven't mentioned is blue paper. Yes, I said blue paper. Some time or other you'll work a place that has paper that is a light blue. I don't know why the paper is blue, although it probably has something to do with glare. The paper is usually of good quality but offers two drawbacks. First, the colors are not as vivid on the blue as they would be on the white. The second is a little more personal. My lightly penciled on-the-fly charts, those of the planned spontaneity variety, would not come over as well. I usually prepare these penciled charts before I get to the location. The audience would be aware that the page is not blue. This is another good reason to set up well in advance of your session. I usually try to get set up the night before the meeting. If I can't do that, I'll try to get into the room as early as possible that morning. In addition, it's one of the questions you will want to ask your contact at the site. *"What color are your flip chart pads?"* It sounds silly, but it's worthwhile.

The Marker

A major tool is the writing instrument itself. There is quite a variety available from pastels to crayons to the popular magic marker.

I'm going to dismiss the variety of crayons and pastels, and concentrate on what we usually call magic markers or just markers. There are all sorts of different sizes, shapes, and points. One brand named Mr. Sketch™ and another manufactured by Dennison, named and packaged like Life Savers™, have scents to them. The blue smells like blueberry, the

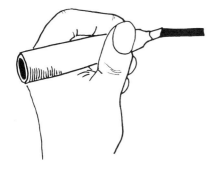

brown like chocolate, the black like licorice, and so on. After working with a number of different markers, I've come to the conclusion that only two brands are acceptable: El Marko™ and Paper Mate™.

Incidentally, it's hard to tell the difference between El Marko™ and Paper Mate™, in quality, price, and longevity. The only difference is that El Marko™ has a squared bottom which keeps the marker from rolling off the table if you set it down. The Gillette people, which manufacture both markers, told me that there is a difference but I can't detect it.

The others have been rejected for a variety of reasons. Some examples: the tip isn't strong enough to withstand my heavy hand and soon looks and writes like a cotton ball; some tips are too long and after a short time fold over; some tips are just too small, or too pointed; or they don't have the ¼-inch beveled edge I consider necessary for legible printing.

It's always interesting to note how reluctant presenters are to use the ¼-inch width. Some of that is due to the uncomfortable way they have to hold the marker. I've never found it uncomfortable or a problem. But it does take a little practice.

I've also had people say that I use 'em up faster because I use the widest segment. *"Rich, that costs money—markers are expensive."* This argument is so silly I'm flabbergasted when someone says this. Consider the cost of a typical session:

- 18–20 particpants' salary and fringes
- Facility, equipment, and supplies
- Presenter/instructor expense
- Program, instrumentation (if purchased)

What percentage of that is a dozen markers?

There are two types of El Marko™ or Paper Mate™ markers: watercolor and permanent. There is no apparent difference in cost and their useful life seems to be the same, if you replace the tops when the marker is not being used. If you don't, the permanent will dry out faster. So, what are the other differences?

The watercolor markers will not bleed through to the next page. On the down side, they tend to be a bit lighter than the permanent markers. By lighter, I mean that the colors are not stark or brilliant. Some, depending on the color, are almost pastel. Permanent markers, on the other hand, will bleed through, although spotty, but the colors are darker. Blacks are black and not dark gray. One last disadvantage of some watercolor markers is the squeaking. They often emit an obnoxious squeal similar to that of a fingernail across a chalkboard.

There is one particular advantage of watercolor markers: the marks will wash out of your clothing. I was in the middle of a presentation when I dropped a black permanent marker on my gray flannel pants. This was just after a participant told me that using permanent markers was risky. Fortunately, that mark came out. A white shirt, however, still has a ¾-inch black mark above the belt line after a half dozen trips through the washer.

Regardless of the minor risks, I still use permanent markers. I prefer the sharp, dark colors to the faded tones of watercolor.

There are many places to buy markers: office supply stores, art shops, drug stores, and super markets. Unless you can get a great discount by buying in quantity, the super market appears to offer the best price. But if you watch the ads that come in the mail, such as the two at the right, you can get a bargain.

The Yard Stick

Another tool which I find extremely useful is a yard stick—a plain old wooden one that you can purchase in any paint store, carpet shop, or hardware store. Many times, such places will give you one. It'll come in handy in many situations.

In a later chapter, I'll talk about storing a yard stick in a carrying tube. If you're going to do this, saw the yard stick off at twenty-seven inches. Notice that this is the width of a standard flip chart page and about all you'll ever need vertically as well. This length will also fit diagonally in most suitcases or bags.

The prime function of the yard stick is to permit you to draw a straight line under a caption or heading. When you do that, you'll very often use red or some other color. You'll find that if the yard stick has been used for a while, the black from the edge of the yard stick (from drawing black lines) will contaminate or color the tip of your marker (a color other than black). If you now use this marker to draw bullets, or print, for example, you'll find that the black will show up on the paper. There are two ways to avoid this problem.

The first method is to use only one side of the yardstick for black, the other side for red or orange. The trouble with this method is that the yardstick doesn't have enough edges for all the colors that you might want to underline with. A better method is to designate certain markers as "liners." You can do that by taking the cap from a dried out black marker and put it on the red (or green or blue) liner. Use the liner only for drawing lines. You'll find that the black will not show up if you hold the "liner" in a consistent manner. Try it. It works.

I also find the yard stick useful in drawing circles. How's that? Using a yard stick, a straight edge, to draw circles? How do you do that?

Well, there are really three easy ways that you can do this. In the first method the yard stick, just the way you got it from the store, is all you need. First determine the diameter of the circle you want to draw, let's say twenty-two inches. Find the center of the chart by counting in on the grid, or measure in $13\frac{1}{2}$ inches (recall that the pad is twenty-seven inches wide) and make a mark. Now place the 11-inch mark (half the desired diameter) on that spot and place a light pencil mark at the beginning of the yard stick and at twenty-two inches. Rotate the yard stick a couple of inches and repeat the process. Keep this up and you'll end up with a lot of marks that can then be linked. I suggest you first link them lightly in pencil and then go over the pencil marks with the marker.

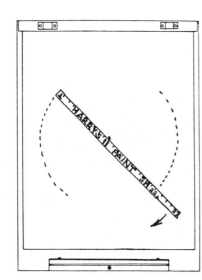

The second method takes a little preparation. However, once it's done you'll not have to do it again. So, it is probably a good investment of time. Take your wooden yard stick and drill a small hole in the middle of the stick at the one-inch mark. The hole should not be larger than $\frac{1}{6}$ of an inch. A starter drill or Yankee drill would be just the right tool for this little job. Now drill similar holes every one or two inches along the yard stick.

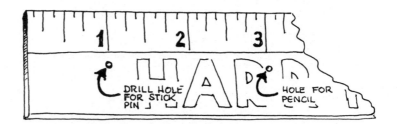

To operate this sophisticated instrument you need a stick pin and a pencil. Stick the pin through the hole at the one-inch mark and put it at the center of your chart. If you're going to draw another 22-inch circle put your sharpened pencil through the hole at the 12-inch mark (12-inch mark because the stick pin is one inch from the end of the yard stick.). Draw your circle by holding the stick pin and rotating the yard stick while keeping the pencil in the hole.

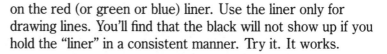

The last of these methods of drawing a circle doesn't require a great deal of effort and is really pretty neat. It's a little device called a yard stick compass manufactured by Griffin Manufacturing Company of Webster, New York. It costs about three or four dollars in your local art supply store. It consists of two small devices with slots into which the yard stick can be inserted. Caps at the top of each device screw down to hold the yard stick in place. One of the devices has a sharp point on the end while the other carries a piece of lead. Positioning the point and rotating the other pencil produces your circle. If you use this little gem, don't try to approximate the positions. Instead, place the device (either one) on the line next to the inch mark you're using.

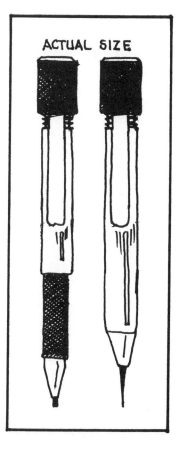

ACTUAL SIZE

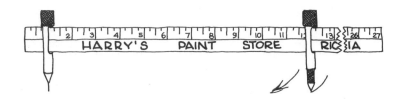

HARRY'S PAINT STORE RICHIA

I call this yard stick compass a gem and I treat it that way. I keep mine in my survival kit in a small box made just for the compass. Not only is the box custom-made, but the compass is cushioned in tissue paper.

These techniques can be used for both predrawn charts and those drawn on-the-fly. You can really wow the participants when you draw a fairly symmetrical circle freehand. It appears freehand to the audience but you've really got those lightly penciled lines to guide you. Another "picky" thing, these circles, but it it makes a difference and that little difference is what will distinguish you from the rest of the crowd.

Pocket Knife

Which brings me to the pocket knife. Its uses are many and obvious; for example, opening boxes of material. Let me move right on to what I think is the most important.

Recall that earlier I suggested you tape your predrawn charts to the pad with transparent tape. Now, in order to remove the charts so that you can use them again, cut them off with the knife. If you try to pull them off, you'll either tear your beautiful chart or end up with a stub of tape. The stub creates problems when you try to roll 'em up. Cut through the tape with a light touch or else you'll cut too deeply into the pad. A small sharpening steel will keep the knife well-honed.

A word of caution. On occasion, you'll have to mount a fresh pad on an easel. When you do, once in a while the holes of the pad will not line up with the screws (posts) on the easel. Please do not use your pocket knife to try and make the holes bigger or otherwise line up the pad. I tried this once. The blade on the knife broke and came flying back, just missing my right eye. It scared the daylights out of me. It's something I'll never try again.

The Survival Kit

I have one other tool which I'd like to share with you, my survival kit. It isn't a sophisticated device, but a school box that's been taped so often it looks awful. I never do a program without it.

My friend Bill Dunphy has a nice nylon zippered case made by Boyt of Iowa Falls, Iowa (515) 648-4626. They make a variety of bags and pocket envelopes for supplies. Bill's case was the 5½- × 9-inch Executive Companion which retails for around forty dollars. It contains: paper clips, rubber bands, single hole punch, pencil sharpener, scissors, stapler with staples, tape dispenser with tape, 6-inch ruler, 6-foot tape measure, combination pen and presenter pointer, business card slot, knife with file, can opener, and screw driver. Note that there aren't any markers.

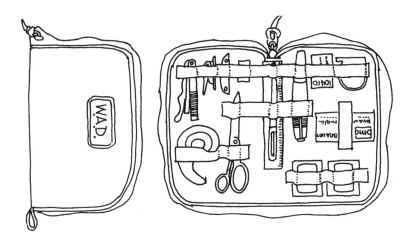

In doing Presentation or Train-the-Trainers programs, I'd mention my survival kit in passing, or not at all. That was a couple of years ago. However, I found myself receiving letters and phone calls from trainers and presenters asking me to tell them what I had in the box. Consequently, I now tell participants what's in the survival kit during the session and have made a photocopy of the list to send to those who request it. So, for what it's worth, here's what's in my survival kit:

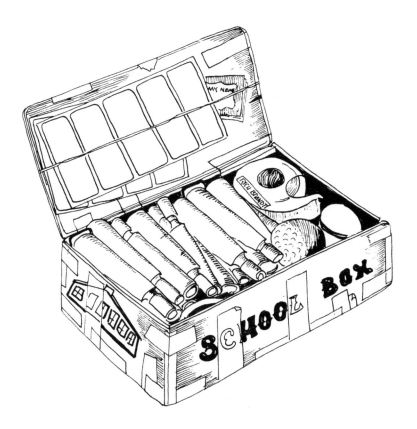

- The yard stick compass. It has already been mentioned.

- Roll of ¾-inch transparent (invisible) tape in a grey plastic dispenser. The tape is used primarily to affix prepared charts to the pad on the easel. Masking tape works, but it looks unprofessional and ugly. When you tape the chart to the top of the pad, tape in three places, each corner, as close to the edge of the page as possible, and in the middle. Anything else creates some problems (bends and folds) in flipping the page.

  Remember to leave a blank page or two between pre-printed charts, so the audience can't see through to the chart underneath.

- Roll of ½-inch double sticky tape in a grey plastic dispenser. The tape is used to attach reveals to appropriate flip charts. I'll address the construction and use of reveals in the next chapter. For those of you who may not recognize the term reveal as we use it, let me explain.

  A reveal is a strip of paper (usually doubled) that covers a point preprinted on a chart. The printing is uncovered or revealed (the strip of paper is torn away) as that item is addressed by the presenter.

- Small role of masking tape to hang charts (after use) on the wall. See the Display Section in Chapter 2.

- Plastic 35mm film canister filled with plastic-headed stick pins. Some fabric-covered walls will not accept masking tape very well. Rather than spending all my time picking up charts and re-taping them, I'll use the pins to stick the charts onto the wall.

  Sometimes nothing works very well in getting the charts up on the wall. The tape won't stick and the pins won't penetrate the wall. That's when I really would like to have about fifty of those clips with stickum that I mentioned earlier.

- Another plastic film canister filled with straight pins. These were added when I did a program in a hotel room where all the walls were covered with drapes. The tape wouldn't hold so I bought a package of pins in the sundry shop and pinned the charts to the drapes.

- Seven-inch pair of scissors. In addition to their multiple uses, you'll need them to cut double-stick tape. Invisible tape can be torn with the serrated edge of the dispenser. However this doesn't work too well with the very small pieces of double-stick tape we'll be using for reveals. You'll have to cut them with the scissors.

- Small one-hole punch. It comes in handy for inserting handouts, articles, and other papers into the three-ring binder that I use for instructor notes.

- Child's pencil sharpener.

- Rexel Little Goliath™ stapler and a box of Tot™ staples to fit.

- Small glue stick.

- Single-edged razor blade wrapped in cardboard.

- Binaca™ breath spray.

- Chap Stick™.

- A nail. I don't remember what I ever did with that.

- Some chalk.

- Golf ball (half white and half green) used in a conflict lecturette.

- Small plastic dispenser full of paper clips.

- Cardboard cut-out of a "thumbs up" sign.

- Whole bunch of markers:
  One each of yellow, brown, purple, and orange. *Two each* of red and green. *All the black and blue I can cram in the box.*

- Luggage tag.

There's a great conference center where you can throw your business card in a basket at the desk when you check in and overnight they'll laminate it and add straps to make it into a luggage tag.

I arrived one session and, as I always do, I threw a business card into the basket. (If you travel a lot you know that you never have enough luggage tags.) I then proceeded to my room. When I got there I noticed a thin layer of grit and dust over everything. I called the desk and asked them to send someone to clean up the place and change the towels. I then went off to set up for the session.

The next morning, on my way to breakfast, I stopped by to pick up my luggage tag. There it was, beautifully laminated, the conference center's name on the reverse side, and under my name, someone had printed, in ink, the word "picky."

Well I thought that was great. The manager didn't and swore that no one on her staff would do such a thing. I told her I wasn't upset, and not to worry about it, but she was almost hysterical. I now use that luggage tag to illustrate that feedback comes in many forms, from many sources. Audiences love the story.

- A lot of small miscellaneous stuff like Life Savers,™ Maalox™ tablets, aspirin, rubber bands, and so on. The sorts of things you tend to collect over the years. You don't know what to do with it, but you don't want to throw it away. I have a tool shed full of stuff like that at home.

- A variety of correction tapes and tools. One of the frustrating things that can happen to a trainer is to look back at an important, complex chart and see an error. It's surprising to some how many mistakes they make, especially those in spelling. We are amazed when single syllable words that we use all the time are wrong.

But we're not the only ones. Read on for a really visible error. Some years ago in Richmond, Virginia (about fifteen miles from my home in Short Pump) a new sea food restaurant opened in a brick house on Broad Street. Broad Street is the main thoroughfare running east and west through town.

The owners decided to paint a sign, two stories high, on the side of the building. Well, the professional ended up with the word "Florida" spelled with two "i's": FLORIDIA. We're talking about letters six feet high. Of course we can blame the sign painter. But thousands of people, including the restaurant owners, looked at that sign as it was being painted. I assure you the sign took more than a couple of days to complete.

Aside from the fact that some of us, myself included, are just poor spellers, there are other things that come into play here. Most of the time when we're drawing a chart we're not focused on writing whole words but on printing individual letters. The closeness and concentration on style and attractiveness also has a bearing. We'll discuss spelling a bit more later on, but right now I'd like to spend some time on making corrections. Let's examine some of the things in the survival kit for making corrections, and how to make them.

Making Corrections

Self-adhesive correction tape of various widths is great. I carry both ⅙-inch and ⅓-inch widths. Their use is fairly obvious. You tape over the portion in error, an extra line or small mistake, and then print over the tape. Depending on the type of marker, you may find a difference in the depth of the color. This is particularly true of red and green.

Various sized self-adhesive labels are useful. Some have borders which must be cut off with a pair of scissors. When you cut off borders, don't cut them all off before you peel off the backing. If you do, you'll spend too much time trying to peel the backing. The use of a label is the same as the tape. The only difference is that you've obviously got to correct a bigger gaffe.

Most of you are familiar with the idea of "cut and paste." This is a procedure where copies of drafts are cut and pasted (taped) together in new sequences with additions or deletions. You can do the same thing with flip charts.

One of the tools in my box is a single-edged safety razor blade. It is wrapped in cardboard, for safety, with a rubber band holding it all together. The razor blade is used to make corrections by cutting out the bad printing or verbiage when the error area is large. At the right is a step-by-step illustration of what to do.

Step 1. Oops! Objectives should come before the process.

Step 2. Cut around the incorrect printing.

Keep cuts angular.

Stay away from the printing, both good and bad.

Step 3. Tape the edges to the sheet underneath.

Step 4. Print corrected copy.

Above, I mentioned making this type of insert with a razor blade. However, I've done the same thing with my pocket knife and, in a rush, haven't bothered to tape the edges. It's fast and it works.

If this chart is one that you want to save and use again, you roll up and take both sheets. However, this may be cumbersome and damage the chart. A more permanent solution is available.

In step two, cut through the sheet underneath at the same time you're cutting out the error. You'll end up with a piece of blank paper the same size as the error removed. Turn the page over and carefully place the blank in the void (hole) left in the original chart. Tape it in place. Not just in spots, but every edge. Turn it over and print the corrected copy. If the cut is very noticeable, fill the cleft by going over it with a soft white pencil. The heavier the paper, the better this technique works.

As you can see, there really isn't anything extraordinary in the items mentioned. Like any other situation, it's a lot easier when you have the right tools. In the next chapter, Design and Technique, we'll look at how to use these tools for best results.

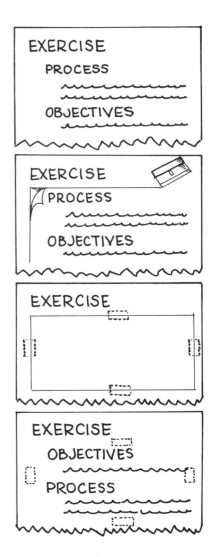

Chapter 4.

Design and Technique

I had a bit of a problem deciding whether or not to combine these two concepts, design and technique. With design, we're looking at structure, content, color, and spacing. With technique, we're examining how to *do* all those things, for example, the actual printing. As you can see I resolved my dilemma in favor of combining the two. I don't think they are really separate components.

Design in flip charts means there's more involved than just information presented in a cute or pretty manner. Good design will add to the receptivity of the content. Thus, design becomes a part of the learning process and is an aid to learning. If receptivity is enhanced, then some barrier to learning and understanding has been removed. The net then, in this area anyway, is that we're ahead of the game.

A basic tenet here is that you've got to put a little thought into your charts before your presentation. I'm not talking about a lot. Even a little bit will make a difference.

Many people think that good design and technique are some magical or God-given gifts. They think these are innate, possessed by only a few people. I won't argue that some people have artistic talent and some do not. But I also believe that there is skill involved, and as such can be learned. If that weren't true, there are a lot of schools and seminars around the country cheating people. I also have evidence that exposure to good technique, with some thought and practice will make a major contribution to professional-looking and effective charts.

About every third time I do a session, someone will ask me if I took drafting lessons. The answer is no. But they do not ask or make a statement about some innate talent. To repeat what I said above, it can be learned.

Now, we're going to examine these areas of design and technique, beginning with printing. If you don't believe you can learn and improve, I suggest you skip this chapter. You probably wasted your money buying this "picky" book.

Printing

Good printing involves four factors:

• Consistency • Motion • Position • Time

Consistency

Consistency refers to the style of printing to be used on a chart. First of all, I would never recommend script on charts unless you've a very plain and a very good handwriting. Even then, I notice that some presenters with outstanding handwriting tend to write too small.

If you decide to print, which I strongly recommend, then stick to block letters, all capitals. Mixing styles and sizes merely adds to the difficulty of printing and legibility.

Assuming that you'll give block letters a try, the next consistency is the slant or angle of the letters themselves. My suggestion is that you assume a slant or style that is easy for you to print at a relatively good rate of speed—and stick with it. I firmly believe that maintaining a particular angle, along with size and style, will help anyone's printing.

Motion

Motion is the second factor for good printing. Let's look at what it means. When you make the strokes, as indicated on the next page, do not labor over them. Make your stroke with a fluid but sharp, crisp movement. If you continue that consistently, a style and confidence will develop. Laboring over the stroke, especially the first, will do a number of things:

• Cause participants to fall asleep or become anxious waiting for you to finish.
• Decrease your eye contact.
• Will not produce a straighter line. It'll probably be even more squiggly.
• Will not provide the right type of practice.

Note that even with the strokes indicated on the next page, there are some options. Experiment with what feels comfortable and what works well for you. Some changes you might consider:

• The "O" as one stroke.   • The "Z" as one stroke.
• The "S" as one stroke.   • The "Q" as two strokes.

Recognize that the basic movement is *down*. Another thing that you may have noticed, is that all letters begin with the left stroke; that is, the left side of the letter is drawn first. The reason for this is to permit proper spacing. It avoids beginning the letter "M" at the right and then finding that it has to be squeezed in order to fit.

Position

The third factor is position and refers both to the letter and to your body or where you stand in relation to the easel.

As you're developing your style, there are some things to think about. For instance, where will you position the cross stroke of letters such as "A" and "H" in regard to height? Similar proportion questions come with such letters as "K," "R," "Y," and others. To be consistent means having that lower portion of the letter at the same place on most of your letters.

The letter "B" presents a bit of a problem. If the cross stroke is too low, the "B" seems out of whack. I tend to make my cross strokes pretty low, yet balance out the letter "B."

Notice the size of the letters on page 35. All of the letters are about 1⅛ inches high, printed with the broad tip of a marker (El Marko™). That size is very visible up to about thirty-five feet—a distance that will accommodate most presentations or seminars. Measure off thirty-five feet and take a look at that distance.

It is not just the size that makes a character or word legible. Line A is certainly bigger (longer) than line B but line B will be more legible in a room of twenty-five participants. This emphasizes the need, or use, of the broad part of the marker.

A colleague, Dick Meyer, is left-handed. He is an outstanding seminar leader. I simply delight in watching him stand, almost behind a chart, and print across his chest, so to speak. Think of the advantages:

- Dick continues to face the participants.
- His body doesn't obstruct the chart.

As a matter of fact, since he's left-handed his arm doesn't even block the view of what he's printing. I think Dick's technique is so marvelous, I tried to print left-handed. Unfortunately, even with a lot of practice, I just couldn't do it. The point of this little tale is that unless you're a Dick Meyer, you've got to think about where you're standing in relation to the chart. You've also got to work on expanding your own style.

The best place to stand is directly in front of the chart, your body centered over the left half, if you're right-handed—6.75 inches from the left margin (just in case you require precision).

The primary reason printing wanders, usually down, is the limited span (the arc) of your arm. If you stand to the side (the left if you're right-handed) you can't reach the farther area of the pad.

*Chapter 4: **Design and Technique***

The argument against this is, *"Rich, you've got your back the participants."* I'm aware of this. Bob Cabot, a colleague and a topnotch presenter/facilitator whom I equate to Carroll's Cheshire Cat (a mammoth vocabulary coupled with marvelous pronunciation and elocution), criticized me for this at a recent instructor training session. The critical difference, I think, is that during that session, I was incorrectly doing a lot of talking while writing.

Notice I said that I was talking. There are some instances, a discussion for example, where you will want to be "out" of it. Having your back to the audience is one way of doing that. You might, for example, throw out a good open-ended question and then turn your back to the group, with a marker poised to record their comments.

But you can't write on the chart with ease if you're standing on either side; unless of course, you're another Dick Meyer. Not only will the printing style be less than it might be, but also your perspective will not lend itself to printing on a straight plane, both horizontally and vertically.

Another common complaint, *"Rich, how do I gracefully print near the bottom of the chart?"* I've got some answers for that question but I can't really say they're graceful. Some things that you might consider:

- Just bend over and print what you have to.

- Kneel down, print, and say a prayer at the same time.

- Pick up the bottom of the pad with the backing.

- Slide the page up to a comfortable height.

- Tip the entire easel away from you.

Time

The final point is time. This is one I have the greatest difficulty with. It's one I hear from a lot of my colleagues and I'm asked about as I travel around the country working with trainers and presenters. The answers are difficult. The reasons are pretty straight forward:

- You don't want your back to the participants longer than is necessary.

- You don't want unnecessary periods of silence blunting a good discussion or thrust.

For legibility, I'm certain that the additional time required is a matter of seconds, four or five per line or comment. That slight difference, that added time, will significantly increase the quality of the printing.

A final point on time has been mentioned before but it's worth repeating. Don't try to write everything. Focus on the key phrase or words. They'll usually occur at the beginning or end of the participants' comments.

A colleague from whom I learned a great deal is the late Jesse Standish. Jesse had the ability to take that extra few seconds so that his on-the-fly printing looked great. He also had the knack of omitting vowels as he printed a key word or phrase and he could do this encoding very quickly.

- Develop—DVLP
- Constant—CNSTNT
- Manager—MNGR

Please note that if the word begins with a vowel it is not left out, as in "ENVRNMNT"

There are a lot of abbreviations that even leave out some of the consonants yet we all recognize and use them:

- Management—MGT
- Communication—COMMO
- Requirement—REQT
- With—W/
- Without—W/O

Just truncating, cutting off the end of a word, will also pick up some time.

- Problem—PROB
- Objective—OBJ
- Organization—ORGAN

Earlier, we spoke of the problem that some of us have with spelling. These abbreviations can help alleviate that problem.

Another way of offsetting the audience's expectations of your spelling ability is through humor. Two ways of doing that are as follows:

Early in the program, when you are, for example, listing the participants' problem inventory or expectations for the session, stop at a particular word and say to them: *"You'll notice as this program proceeds that I'm not a very good speller. It doesn't bother me; I hope it doesn't bother you. I subscribe to a comment attributed to Mark Twain who said, 'Anyone who can only spell a word one way isn't very creative.' I tend to be very creative."*

The second, which I've not used, is to hang a flip chart sheet on the wall, before the beginning of the program, which has all the letters of the alphabet on it. Tell the audience that if they notice a word misspelled during the session, just add one of these letters or substitute for one I've misused.

The one area that you have to be extremely careful with is spelling participants' names correctly. I'm convinced that participants are very sensitive to this. It's worth some extra effort.

In wrapping up this section on printing, the key items are:

- Settle on a style.
- Take that extra time.
- Practice.

Color

I can't say enough about the use of color in a flip chart. The correct use of color in charts can make a difference in the dynamics of a presentation and the acceptance of the content. Any color can be good or bad depending on how or where it is used. Similarly, a great chart can suffer from the poor use of color.

Look at the charts below from a distance of six to eight feet. You can see the difference. Normally, people will have some difficulty reading a chart printed entirely in red. Red should only be used as an accent color—bullets, underlines, arrows, the minutes on a timing chart, and emphasis circles. Key words may be written in red when everything else is in black or blue.

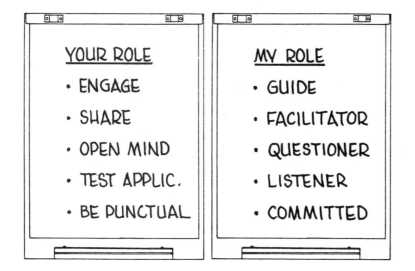

The colors with the greatest visibility are black, blue, and green, in that sequence. The Optical Society of America did a survey of 21,060 observations in twenty-six investigations. The study revealed that blue ranked as the most pleasing color. Red was ranked as the second most pleasing color. But pleasing and visibility are two different things. Red and orange should be used only as accents. Avoid purple, brown, pink, and especially yellow, for any type of general printing.

Using colors in combination on a chart is very effective. Two colors are better than one. Three aren't bad if done carefully and with purpose. More than three tend to be a bit much. The audience may have difficulty picking up accents or emphasis. Certain combinations of colors are not conducive to good contrast and visibility:

Avoid

- red and green
- orange and blue
- yellow and any color

Good Contrasts

- red with black or blue
- blue and black (and vice versa)
- green with black (and vice versa)

Think about these combinations of colors if you have a series of charts. A sense of organization and flow can be enhanced through proper use of color combinations. Viewers looking at the charts at the top of the next page have an immediate sense that these three charts are all tied together. Would they have this sense if each chart were drawn in a different color? Maybe they would, but the organization is obvious if the colors are coordinated from chart to chart.

Color can be very helpful in making assignments for various exercises. Not just for round robin role plays as shown on page 9, but also for team and task force assignments. Printing all the names in one color, as shown in the example at the left, can heighten the desired clarity.

The next time you're drawing charts, whether on-the-fly or prior to a session, take a minute to think about the color you're going to use—not only with the chart you're working on, but also with the one you've just finished and the one that'll come next. Ask the question *"How can I use color in order to enhance understanding?"*

TASK FORCE ASSIGNMENTS

TEAM 1.	TEAM 2.	TEAM 3.
ROOM B.	ROOM D.	ROOM F.
ROGER	SUE	TOM
RUTH	SAM	TESS
RICK	SILAS	TILLY
REGINA	SALLY	TIM
RON	SEAN	TERRY

RECONVENE @ _____

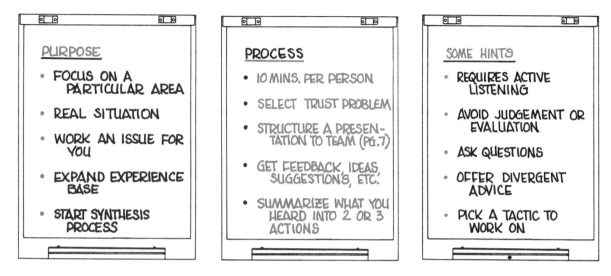

Bullets

In the previous section I used the term "bullets." They're to highlight certain points or distinguish between different items. The term bullet specifically refers to the round dot. However, asterisks, squares, arrows, and dashes all fall under the same general heading. That's the way we'll deal with them in this book.

Why use bullets? Why not just number the items as they are offered or presented? Let's examine some of the alternatives.

One of the things you could do is to pre-number the items as in the chart at the right. Note that there is an immediate expectation that participants must come up with six advantages. If they don't come up with six, they've failed as a group. What if they come up with seven? Well, that's probably all right. The implication is that the presenter doesn't know his or her stuff.

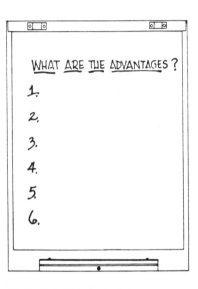

How about numbering them as you go along? That shouldn't be too bad, eh? No, it's not too bad, but still has a minor drawback: people naturally tend to rank or prioritize items as they are numerically sequenced. While this tendency may not be so strong as the items are written, it is much more so afterward (the next day perhaps) when you've taped the chart to the wall.

One obvious way out is to avoid numbers altogether. The exceptions would be those processes in which items should/ must be prioritized, or executed, in a particular sequence. An example would be the Instruction Giving Model at the right. Here, we want each item of the model given in sequence for definite reasons. We would not, for example, want the individual assignments made except where indicated in the sequence.

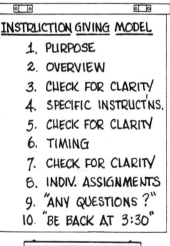

The size of the bullet depends on the size of the letters printed on the chart. Most of the printed letters on a chart are about 1⅛ to 1¼ inches high. For that size, the bullet should not be larger than ¾ of an inch in diameter or less than ½ inch. Merely touching the tip of the marker to the pad appears indecisive or ambiguous. Is it a key point? Well, let 'em know it.

How to draw that bullet for the best chance of symmetry? I've tried a few different ways, not many. After all, how many different ways can there be to draw a bullet? What works for me is to draw a quick circle with the small tip of the marker and then fill it in. This is fast and I get more consistency in size, especially when working with gridded paper. Some do this, but don't fill in the circle.

There are a lot of things you can use other than circles. We've mentioned some of them already—arrows, asterisks, and boxes. John Humphrey, Chairman and CEO of the Forum Corporation, as well as a superb presenter/facilitator, uses something I can only describe as a pretzel. I've seen others who merely use the dash or check quite effectively. Regardless of what you use, be consistent within a set of charts that will all be viewed at the same time. This consistency conveys that sense of organization and thought you have put into the presentation.

Balance and Symmetry

A recurring area for improvement with charts is the one dealing with balance and symmetry. We've all seen a variation of the sign that proclaims "Plan Ahead" with the part of the word or letters falling off the end of the sign. Unfortunately, it happens quite often, not only with charts drawn on-the-fly but even with those predrawn. The latter is usually an obvious blunder to the participants. It says, *"Yes, I screwed up my spacing but you weren't important enough for me to redo the chart."* What a way to establish rapport with a group!

Once again, the use of the gridded paper is an advantage. It permits you to quickly count boxes (one-inch) and align various items. This is true of charts drawn on-the-fly, such as organization charts and flow charts, where positioning is particularly important. A few pencil marks to indicate angles and position will help enormously.

We all draw many charts, not just on-the-fly, but spontaneously. Many of these charts involve information set in boxes. Earlier I spoke of printing first and then drawing the box around the word or words. For planned spontaneity, you can draw some lightly penciled lines or marks to tell you exactly where that box and the printing within it should be placed. The Communications Process at the right (drawn on-the-fly) is a good example of where this is essential. The chart has an awful lot on it—lines, boxes, printing. Space is at a premium. Without some penciled guidelines, this chart could be a mess.

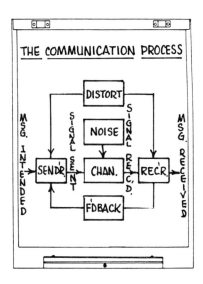

The grid is also helpful in determining printing spaces. After some practice, you'll realize the width of most of your printed letters. If a question comes up about fitting a word on the rest of a line, a quick count will give you a pretty good idea of whether the answer is yes or no.

As you practice, you'll discover refinements that make your spacing estimates more accurate. Some that I use:

- I know that most of my letters with the space between them are a fraction less than an inch.

- I also know an "I" does not take as much space while an "M" or "W" takes a bit more.

- I can pick up some space with a "T" depending on the letters before and after: "AT" vs. "WT."

- Letters such as "E," "F," "H," and "L" are easy to vary by making the horizontal strokes shorter or longer.

These little adjustments permit me to space my words for more balance and symmetry on the chart.

Balance also has to take the entire chart into consideration. Look at the chart at the right. You'll say it is top heavy. I agree. The presenter, instead of planning, just started print-ing.

Imbalance should never occur with charts that are predrawn (but it does) and can be avoided with those drawn on-the-fly. *"But Rich, I can't say exactly how many comments I'll get from the participants!"* That's true. But you'll know the range. You'll know that you seldom get twelve to fifteen items, and more likely six to eight.

Let's say you've decided on six to eight items. If about six inches for the top margin and title are allowed, print the first comment on the eighth line from the top of the paper. Now we have twenty-eight inches (lines) left for the seven remaining comments. Dividing twenty-eight by seven, each comment should be four inches (lines) apart. If you don't get eight, no problem; but what if you now get nine items? Print the ninth item between the first and second. My preference would be to allow for only six items. After printing the first item, space five lines apart and start interspersing earlier.

With some practice, you'll quickly get a sense of how much space you'll need. The point is to think ahead and space accordingly. If you know you're only going to get three key points, don't print them all on the top three inches of the page.

Obviously, there are some situations where you'll easily fill up one, two, three, or more pages. An example would be listing a problem inventory from participants at the beginning of a session. A group of twenty to twenty-four participants could require three pages.

One of the problems is trying to capture too much. Recall the earlier caution to select only key words or phrases. Recently, working with a colleague, we alternated recording management challenges. The participant group numbered twenty-one, which means we each would record about a dozen comments (some will give two). Well, I was able to get all of mine on one page. My co-leader used three sheets.

You've got to listen. Remember what I said in the section on printing. The key point or phrase will generally come at the beginning or end of someone's comment. That's all you want to write. It is also very important to use their words . . . don't paraphrase.

Someone will quickly say, *"Well, Rich, what's two more sheets of paper?"* It's not the cost; it's the time and disruption of pulling charts off and taping them up. It's also the wall space. Time, continuity, wall space—all important considerations.

One thing we haven't addressed directly is how much should be on a particular chart. There is no hard rule such as, *"No more than six points should be on any flip chart!"* However, restraint should be a guiding principle.

If your printing isn't the greatest in the world, a lot of copy will look cluttered. Yet there are times when clutter is totally consistent with the situation. Writing all over a chart, in the margins, with arrows going every which way, often indicates a good discussion. Some suggestions along these lines:

- A lot of white space makes the chart look cleaner and printed material easier to read.

- Don't begin printing right at the edge of the paper. Keep a margin of at least three or four inches. If the points consist of a word or two, a seven or eight-inch margin may be appropriate.

- Whatever margin you leave on the left, try to leave a similar margin on the right. However, the right margin can be a bit smaller without loss of balance.

- The margin at the bottom of the page should be a bit larger than the margin at the top of the page. It provides a sense of stability, a base.

- Indent sub-items and distinguish them from the major point with a different bullet. For example, if you use a round dot for the major point, use an asterisk for the sub-item.

- Keep all items, major or sub, lined up vertically.

- Sub-items provide an appropriate place to change color. If the major point was printed in black with a green dot, the sub-item may be printed in green with a black asterisk.

Sometimes there is just too much to present. One page isn't going to be enough unless the printing is small and really crammed. In this case, simply use two, or even three, pages. Below are two examples of this type of situation.

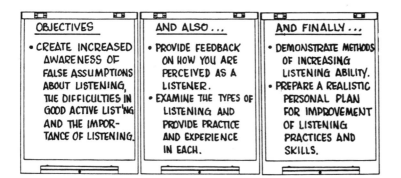

The above Rube Goldberg cartoon copyright by King Features Syndicate, Inc. Reprinted with special permission of King Features Syndicate, Inc.

The top example, on the preceding page shows predrawn charts, using three easels, citing the objectives of Brandt Management Group's two-day seminar/workshop, "The Business of Listening." As you might imagine, the charts are not all uncovered at the same time. They are uncovered one at a time as the first item on the chart is presented. The second example is also from BMG's listening program. It demonstrates how a large illustration can be presented with two easels.

And finally, I don't want to say that every chart should have a title, but I'll wager that it's 99 $^{44}/_{100}$ percent true. The audience likes to be kept in sync with what's going on. Titles help do that. It becomes particularly important if you're going to put that chart up on the wall. A title gives it impact.

Furthermore, the title is another way that you can add some color, individuality, or pizzazz—something other than a straight line. Some examples are at the left.

Just as in other topics, the key to successful, well-balanced charts is just a little thought on what you're about to do. Try it—it works!

Non-Verbals

A lot of my colleagues seem to shy away from non-verbals when they use flip charts. They can be extremely effective and you don't have to be an artist to use them. The questions to ask yourself are, *"What is it I'm trying to accomplish? Is it art? Is it a change of pace, a little humor, learning, or all of the above?"* It's probably not something that will hang in the Metropolitan Museum of Art. Take the chart at the left. I could say the words, but the impact and retention wouldn't be the same.

Stick figures are great, simple to draw, and show a variety of actions. As simple as the strokes are, a message is being transmitted. The message is what's important.

A takeoff on the happy face is also easy to accomplish. Just a line or squiggle can change a happy face to a grouch. The chart at the right is one I use when speaking about reentry into the work place. *"If you left the office looking like this . . . and you come in tomorrow morning looking like this . . . well, people are . . ."* Those figures can be drawn as fast as you are talking about them.

Variations on the happy face can be found all over. Find, or design, something simple, something that you like, and that you can draw quickly. Use it on a variety of situations, but don't overdo it in a presentation. An occasional fuzzy-face is great but too many fuzzies are too much.

Timing charts are a good place to insert non-verbals. Several examples are shown at the right. A template for the cuckoo clock can be found in Appendix B. However, I'm sure you can come up with some of your own.

A non-verbal which is effective and has wide application is the thumbs-up, or thumbs-down, sign. It can be used in "Do's and don'ts," or "What did he do well? What didn't he do well?" I'm sure you can figure out some other uses.

For those of you who are thinking, *"I can't draw a thumbs-up sign,"* I have one for you. On page 81, in Appendix B, is a thumbs-up sign in a size that is appropriate for most flip charts. I suggest you photocopy the page and then glue it to some stiff cardboard. Cut it out and you're all set. If you need a smaller one, take it to a quick printing shop and have them reduce it.

As I mentioned on page 28, my thumbs-up cut-out fits in my survival kit. One other point and we'll move on. On page 51, I'll talk about combinations, predrawn information, and printing on-the-fly. The two charts pictured at right are used in that way. The thumbs-up sign, thumbs-down sign, and title are predrawn. The points are added on-the-fly.

Houses, boxes, suns, stars—try 'em all. As you experiment, your style and repertoire will grow and enhance your charts.

Reveals

I've mentioned reveals, sometimes referred to as "strip charts," a bit earlier. Let's take a look at them in some detail. Reveals are a tremendous tool for the presenter. A reveal is a cover-up for predrawn material. It has some dynamite advantages you ought to consider.

- It permits you to be in sync with what you're talking about.

- It's faster than writing it on-the-fly. If you need a minute here and there, this is the way to pick it up.

- It provides a mild change of pace.

- It'll probably look better and neater than on-the-fly.

- It hints that you're a pro who thought enough of the session to do some preparation.

There are essentially two types of reveals, although the first has a number of variations.

In the first type, the bottom of the page is brought up to cover the points on the same page. The problem with this technique, at least my problem, is that the page ends up with fold marks, which I don't like for my charts. Some instructors do the same thing but without the tape. What they do is hold the page up in place and then move (slide) it down to reveal the next point. The difficulty here is that your become rooted to the easel. Imagine the discomfort if one of the early points generates a good discussion. You're stuck.

Another minor disadvantage of folding over the same sheet is that the printing will show through the back of the page. This is especially true if you use permanent markers.

To avoid being rooted to one spot, use masking tape. The masking tape, either doubled over on itself (hidden) or just taped across the edge (messy), holds the bottom of the page over its contents. So the bottom of the page is attached temporarily to the top of the same page. The title is usually not covered up. As each point is addressed, and the instructor is about to go to the next point, he or she unsticks the masking tape, moves the paper down, and resticks it to the chart just below that point.

Here are some hints on doing this. First, transparent tape doesn't work too well for this. It tends to be too permanent, while the masking tape is easier to remove and remains tacky longer. Second, doubling the masking tape over on itself allows the tape to hide in between. It's best to use two pieces, one in each corner, as opposed to one piece in the middle.

Another method of accomplishing this type of reveal is to use one large piece of paper to cover all the points. The entire sheet is moved down as points are uncovered and discussed. This is particularly effective if the points are different lengths, more than one line, for example. If you try this, remember to double the paper so that the printing won't show through.

A second technique is to cover the various points with strips of paper. Sounds easy, doesn't it? But, I've seen more than one marvelous presenter have problems with this method. So let me share with you some ideas to make the technique effective.

- **Double up the strip that you're going to use.** Even 26-pound paper shows through a little bit. Doubling up, just folding it over on itself, eliminates the audience's squinting, trying to read what's underneath the reveal.

- **For best results, don't use masking tape.** Instead, use the two-sided (or double-sided) sticky tape I mentioned in my survival kit. It comes in a half-inch size and should last a long time. But a caution: don't use more than a $\frac{1}{4}$ of an inch; $\frac{1}{8}$ of an inch is even better. (Remember that earlier I said it is very difficult to tear off such a small section. It's best to use a pair of scissors.) I watched and laughed (isn't that bad?) as a good colleague tore off his first reveal and ripped his chart in half. All you want to do is keep it up there until you're ready to rip it off. You don't want it to last 'til the turn of the century.

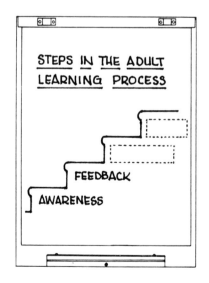

One method suggested to me for attaching the reveal to the page was to glue the sticky portion of Scotch Post-It Notes™ to the strip. I tried this about three or four times but never could get it to work the way I wanted it to. The reveals would fall off at the slightest movement. It's too bad because it would have been a great time saver—just stick 'em back on the chart, no cutting little pieces of double sticky tape.

Notice I said "rip it off." Don't make a project of removing the reveal. It'll have the same effect as laboring to draw a line under a key point. In a word from my colleague Sarah Risher: *"Boring."*

- **Make each stacked (one on top of the other) reveal the same size regardless of the length of the lines.** In the chart at the right the items are not stacked so the length of the reveal is not a factor. If you have an item that takes two (or more) lines, it has to be wider, but the length remains consistent. It's the same principle mentioned on page 20 in drawing boxes.

A SMALL PIECE OF
DOUBLE-SIDED TAPE
TO PREVENT CURLING

- **Tape or glue the inside bottom corners of the reveal** (where you've folded the reveal over on itself) to prevent it from curling up and being too obvious.

- **Consider the length of the reveal.** If it is more than twelve inches long, you might tape the center—to attach it to the chart and to keep the fold together.

- **If you're using paper with the light blue grid, make the reveal from the same paper.** Then try to line up the reveal with the lines on the paper. Again, a minor, almost insignificant point but . . .

Pictured below and on the next page are two effective ways to use reveals that incorporate printing on the reveal itself. The one with a high jump bar is used in a Train-the-Trainers session. About halfway through the week we say, *"We're raising our expectations."* The reveal, when lowered, shows the bar at a higher level. In the second example two reveals are used. "Management" when removed becomes "influence" and the blank reveal is stripped to complete the definition.

Reveals can be used in many ways to enhance your presentation. Think about it and see what you can do. But, like anything else, reveals can be overdone.

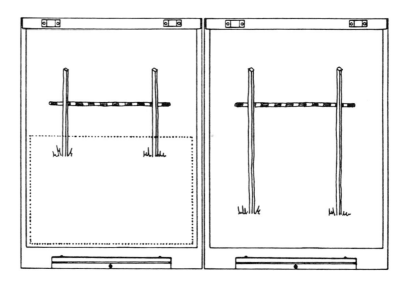

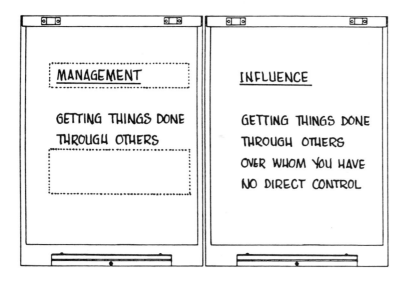

Combinations

Another way to change pace and have an impact is to combine predrawn material with that drawn on-the-fly. An obvious example is the vote chart illustrated on page 10. Many times you'll see the title predrawn, a basic example of combining the two methods. The technique of combining predrawn and on-the-fly information can be extended further. Notice the two examples at the right and the one on the next page.

Here in the top chart, the major captions are predrawn and then, as they are addressed, the subheadings are added (shown in green). In this example they show the managerial functions necessary to achieve the results.

On the next chart, the title and target (the objective) are predrawn. The arrows and captions (both in green) for each are added to show how we're going to get there.

The example on the next page is a bit different from those on the preceding page. It involves non-verbals, a bit of levity, and a cut-out. Where the characteristics of feedback are printed, on-the-fly, the chart has been cut out. Those words are actually printed on the sheet of paper under the predrawn chart, indicated by the dotted lines. (This is similar to the correction technique mentioned on page 31.) There is no need to redraw the chart each time, as would be necessary for the two charts on the right. Cut through the four or five pieces of transparent tape holding the two sheets in place. Throw away the sheet on which you printed on-the-fly, the one underneath. Roll up the predrawn chart (the one with the cut-out) and you're ready for the next session.

I could do the same thing, in any of these three examples, with reveals. However, change of pace and spontaneity do add to the impact.

Look at your own charts. I'm certain you can come up with some clever ideas where combinations of predrawn and on-the-fly material will add to the impact and retention of your information.

Notes

There are two aspects to consider: notes to yourself that are printed on the chart itself, and the notes of your presentation. Let's examine the first of these two.

Writing lightly penciled notes on the flip chart itself is an old trick that most presenters use. The notes should not be some doodling or some remark written just anywhere on the chart. With some thought and planning, they can be extremely useful, especially the first time out with a new presentation or program. So, here are some hints on how to optimize this helpful technique:

- A common mistake is to make the notes too small. Presenters always have a fear that the audience will see the notes. Maybe that is a problem. I don't think so. The problem occurs when you, the presenter, can't see them. That's even worse. Recall that earlier we said large thin letters are harder to see than short fat lines. The same principle is true here. The diffusion of large thin lines makes it more difficult for the audience to see and easier for you to read at a short distance. Print your notes lightly, in pencil, in letters ½-inch high. Don't print your entire presentation, just key words.

- There is a natural tendency to print the notes alongside the related point on the chart. That seems logical enough. However, it's awkward to have to bend over to read them. Place your notes as high as you can. Separate them somehow, a two-inch line for example, so you'll know which goes next.

- There are occasions when the note should rightly be where you're going to print. This would be on a chart that is to be drawn on-the-fly, noting what to print and where to print it. However, be careful not to print over some notes that you're going to use a few minutes later. I'm embarrassed to say that I have done this, though not very often.

- Reproduce your flip charts, word for word, in your notes. When that chart is up there and you're talking about a particular point, the audience will be focused mainly on the chart. That makes it very easy to glance at your presentation notes for the next point, rather than read the chart.

Another aspect of your notes, in conjunction with flip charts, is to indicate easel sequence. We'll discuss this topic, and finding your charts in the next section. A sample of my notes will be included.

Chapter 5.

Mechanics

Orchestration

Orchestration refers to the relationship of chart to chart by position and content. It requires some thought about the objectives of the unit or presentation and how the chart will reinforce them. If you consistently use only one easel, consider this section. Opportunities abound for greater impact through orchestration.

A key item here is synchronization of the visual with your spoken word. A frequent behavior, even among very experienced presenters, is not flipping a chart when they are finished with it. Not keeping visuals (all of them, not just flip charts) in sync with the presentation can cause confusion, frustration, and worse, even animosity.

I mentioned previously the idea of keeping two or three blank pages between your preprinted ones. Synchronization is one of the reasons. If you don't have a blank, you'll have to expose a chart that you may not be ready for just yet.

Orchestration is keeping current charts in view and doing that with clout. For example, set up a chart on the left-most easel which may have four or five key points to be revealed one at a time. The remaining charts are used to expand on each point as it is revealed.

Orchestration also refers to the mix of charts: predrawn and on-the-fly. That mix changes pace, so necessary in adult learning. The presenter who does nothing but flips charts and reads from them is . . . boring. I'm finding that as I redo my teaching notes, I'm using less predrawn charts and doing more on-the-fly. This provides more spontaneity with less of a canned approach to the topic.

Here again, is the blank paper available when you need it? Is it on the right easel? Can you find the predrawn chart to be addressed next?

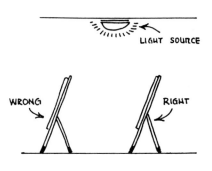

Another aspect of orchestration has to do with the physical position of your easels. The first consideration should be the position of the easels in relation to the lights in the room. Unfortunately, sometimes there isn't a great deal we can do about the lighting. Notice the illustration at the right. Try to position the easels so that they are behind the lights, not in front of them.

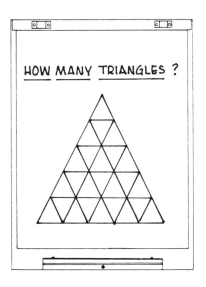

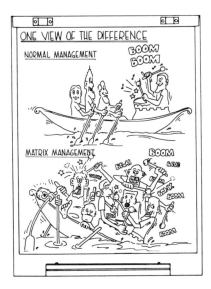

When working with a video screen, there is very often competition for viewing space. Where do I put the easels in relation to the screen? Too often I see presenters place the video screen in the middle of the charts even though the video will only be used for five or ten minutes. Don't permit that five or ten minutes to dictate the setup for a morning's presentation. Place the video screen at the side of an end easel, left or right. Ask the audience to position themselves so that they can see the video portion. When it is finished, move the screen out of the way.

A last point on orchestration has to do with using humor as a change of pace. Flip charts lend themselves very nicely to this activity. Puzzles, such as the one on the left, lighten the climate of a particularly heavy session. Special attention must be given to the timing of such visual breaks. The best time would be at the beginning of a unit or half day. Never interrupt the flow of an exercise/debrief, for example, unless the humorous chart, puzzle or cartoon provides a very direct and obvious analogy.

Reproducing Flip Charts

Reproducing flip charts or machine-prepared charts is another issue. Many organizations use reproductions because they are supposed to look better; they standardize the presentation regardless of the presenter; they avoid the problem of poor printing, and of course sets of charts can be produced in volume, among other likely reasons.

There are two ways chart reproduction can be accomplished: they can be redrawn or put through some machine or mechanical process. We'll examine one at a time these different methodologies, their advantages, and disadvantages.

If charts are to be redrawn, you can either do it yourself or have someone else do it. If you draw them yourself, you're in control; color, balance, and last minute changes are in your hands. For better or worse, you're responsible for the finished product. If you have someone else draw them, there may be a problem in communicating exactly what you want.

Some time ago I was delivering a week-long management seminar for a *Fortune* 500 company. I had contracted to do four seminars a year. Because of scheduling difficulties, I had not drawn any of the charts before the first session, but I knew I had enough time to draw them the day before. After that, I'd save them for subsequent sessions.

On Sunday morning I arrived at the seminar site and began drawing charts. The client saw me and suggested that drawing charts should be left to the seminar administrator, another consultant hired to put things together. The client suggested I give my notes (remember, my charts are reproduced in my notes) to the administrator, and I did. Well, about an hour later I walked in to see how the seminar administrator was doing. The printing and the use of color were great. However, her charts also included my oral notes in bold color. I'm talking about the ones that would ordinarily be in light pencil. You can imagine how she felt when I pointed out the problem.

The point of this little tale is that if you're going to have someone else draw charts for you, you've got to tell them exactly what you want the charts to look like. Don't abbreviate if you want a word spelled out. Indicte exact color, indentation, bullets, titles, and underlining.

If you give the charts to an outside professional, a sign painter, the chances are very good that unless you tell him or her otherwise, the charts will be drawn on posterboard (cardboard). You may or may not have considered posterboard. It has some advantages and disadvantages:

On the plus side are such items as:

- They tend to be more permanent. They should, with a minimum of care, last longer than 26-pound paper.

- You can stand them up on an easel.

- The color, unavailable from mechanical processes, can be used to advantage.

- Posterboard gives a professional touch which may be desirable for the type of presentation or audience.

On the minus side are these items:

- Professionally-drawn charts on posterboard are a bit expensive. The price varies considerably, but a single 27- × 34-inch chart will run no less that thirty-five dollars.

- There's a certain awkwardness in switching or changing charts, with a possibility of knocking them all over. One way to avoid this is not to try putting them back on the easel, behind the others. Just drop them on the floor at your side.

- It's extremely difficult to keep 'em in sync unless you have blank posterboard at the points where you'll need them.

- Where do you write? At thirty-five dollars plus per chart you sure don't want to write on the posterboard. You might try a flip chart next to the posterboard easel.

- They're difficult to display, that is, to hang on the wall.

- Posterboard can be difficult to transport or ship safely.

Redrawing will not be feasible if you need many sets of the charts. There are some ways to reproduce your charts mechanically. The difficulty with machine-prepared charts is the balance between cost and quality. There are basically three processes. Let's look at them.

Photographic

This process provides the best quality and detail but it is also the most expensive. In order to reproduce a chart, a negative has to be made. The cost for the negative is around eight dollars. Once the negative is made you can make as many copies as you need. For a 27- $\times$ 34-inch black and white chart, the cost is about thirty dollars. The finish, although not very shiny, does have a slight sheen. This will sometimes cause a glare problem, but it is minimal.

One big advantage is that you can take an $8\frac{1}{2}$- $\times$ 11-inch original (or any size for that matter) and blow it up. The down side is that small imperfections also get magnified. If you're going to try photographs, make the original as large as possible, perhaps a flip chart page.

Xerography

Xerography is also available at about ten dollars per copy. The copy is also of high quality but can only be 24 inches wide (at least here in Richmond at this time). That three inches really isn't a problem in most cases. I just like all my charts to be the same size. Like the photographic process, the resulting copy is black and white. However, because of the nature of the xerographic process, the black isn't very dark or intense.

Enlargement is also available with xerography, but the maximum enlargement available in one pass is 104 percent, about double. This means that to go from an $8\frac{1}{2}$- $\times$ 11-inch original to flip chart size will require three passes with the accompanying additional cost and magnification of imperfections. Depending on the quality of the equipment, you'll also get the old "copy of a copy" product.

Diazo

The diazo, or blueprint, process is the least expensive if you want to make more than one or two copies. The process requires a tracing. The tracing is the drawing on a light paper very similar to tissue paper and commonly called drafting paper. To make a tracing from your original costs about thirty-five dollars. Once the tracing is obtained, additional copies cost about one dollar each. The resulting copy is either blue or black on white. People will tell you that it's on white but it really isn't. There's a faint hue of blue or gray on the background.

Of the three processes, the diazo has the poorest quality. However, I'm speaking quality in relation to the other two processes. The improvements in the technology over the past few years have made diazo quite acceptable. Unlike the photographic method, diazo and xerography will not produce a real dark black or blue.

These machine-produced charts have their purpose and if you need them in volume and can afford them, go ahead and use them. They can be produced in any drafting/blueprint shop. Because of the processes, however, I think most of these types of charts are lifeless. Here are some easy ways to overcome the blahs of these charts.

- Don't title any of the charts. Let the presenter or seminar leader print the title in a contrasting color, such as red.

- The same is true for underlining, bullets, and other accents.

- If you don't have a professional around to do the printing, use some mechanical device. The simplest is rub-on-letters. If that's not good enough, there are more sophisticated processes available. Among these are Leroy™ and Kroy™. The Leroy™ requires very little skill but a little practice. The lettering uses stencils and an ink stylus. Kroy™ is totally automatic, a photographic process that comes out with adhesive strips. After all, if you're going to spend the bucks to have them reproduced, do a good job with them.

- Pay attention to all the items we're talking about in this book, such as size, balance, and symmetry.

I've seen mechanically reproduced charts that were terrible. It amazes me that companies will go to a lot of expense and still produce poor charts.

If you don't want the presenter to have to add these accents by hand, there are some other options. You can buy rolls of adhesive dots in a wide variety of colors. Both Avery and Dennison sell a box of 1,000 ¾-inch dots for about four and a half dollars. That should be enough to last you for a long time. They are uniform in size and color and thus, consistent with the machine prepared chart. Lines can also be applied this way. Use the kind that are purchased for graphs and bar diagrams. If the colors of the dots and the lines aren't pretty similar, use two different colors. You should be able to find both of these items in any art supply shop, drafting shop, and in most stationery stores.

Remember that the charts don't have to be mechanically produced in order to use these manufactured dots and lines. They work well with your hand drawn charts also.

There is one last thing regarding reproducing flip charts. Most of the personal computers have graphics software available, programs that print different lettering styles and a variety of graphs and pie charts. How would Old English look to your prospect? The combination of this new tool, the personal computer, and the three processes mentioned above offer some outstanding possibilities for innovative and smashing flip charts.

How to Find Your Charts

There probably isn't a one of you reading this who hasn't lost a chart at one time or another. This section will show you how to avoid this in the future.

Some years ago, a very talented colleague, Sarah Risher, and I were teaching a session for the U.S. Navy. The developers had set this course up with five easels. How about that! Five easels! During the session, she had to show some slides. As my colleague began moving the easels so that participants could see the screen, a half dozen men jumped up to help her. After the slide presentation, they again jumped up to put the easels back in place, after which she continued her presentation. But, she couldn't find her charts; the easels were not put back in the right sequence.

So, the first thing you want to do when using multiple easels at a session, is to number them. Put a small piece of masking tape, an inch or two, on the side edge of each easel. Put it up near the top, same place for each easel. Now, with a black marker, number each one. There are all sorts of ways easels can be switched. Numbering them is your insurance against losing your material.

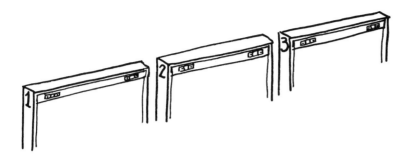

Now, assuming that's squared away and you've put 'em up where you want them, how do you find the one you want? Here are five ways which can be used singularly or, in most cases, in combination:

Mark your notes in some manner. We spoke of reproducing the entire chart in your notes in the section on Orchestration. On the following page is a copy of a page from one of my teaching notes. (It's been reduced slightly, the actual size is 8 $\frac{1}{2}$- $\times$ 11-inches, and the color highlights aren't evident.) You'll note that immediately above the chart itself is a small square with a number. The number indicates the easel on which that chart will be found, or will be drawn on-the-fly.

Marking your notes in this manner also assists you in preparation. It tells you on which easel to place the chart as you set up. In addition, it indicates where you need a blank page for one that'll be drawn on-the-fly.

A word of caution: never draw an on-the-fly chart on the page before one of your predrawn ones—one of those that you labored over. The bleeding from the on-the-fly chart may mark up your predrawn one. This is another place where you want an extra sheet of paper between the two.

When you are drawing your charts prior to a presentation you'll have the same problem. Unless you have an unlimited supply of flip chart pads, put a blank under the page you're printing on. I refer to this as my "bleeder" page. When you finish the chart move the bleeder page under the next blank, and so on.

The note format on the following page is one I've found helpful and evidently other organizations agree. I receive frequent requests to observe and time their programs and then write teaching notes for their presenters and trainers. The notes are hand printed (as shown) and include suggested flip charts.

A second method of finding a chart is to put a tab on the chart, or on the one in front of it. The tab can be made by folding over a piece of masking tape. Mark the tape with some identifier, a number or a word, so that you'll know what it is.

21. 4:45 – 5:10 (25)   <u>PROBLEM SOLVING MODEL</u>

LET'S LOOK AT A MODEL WHICH HELPS

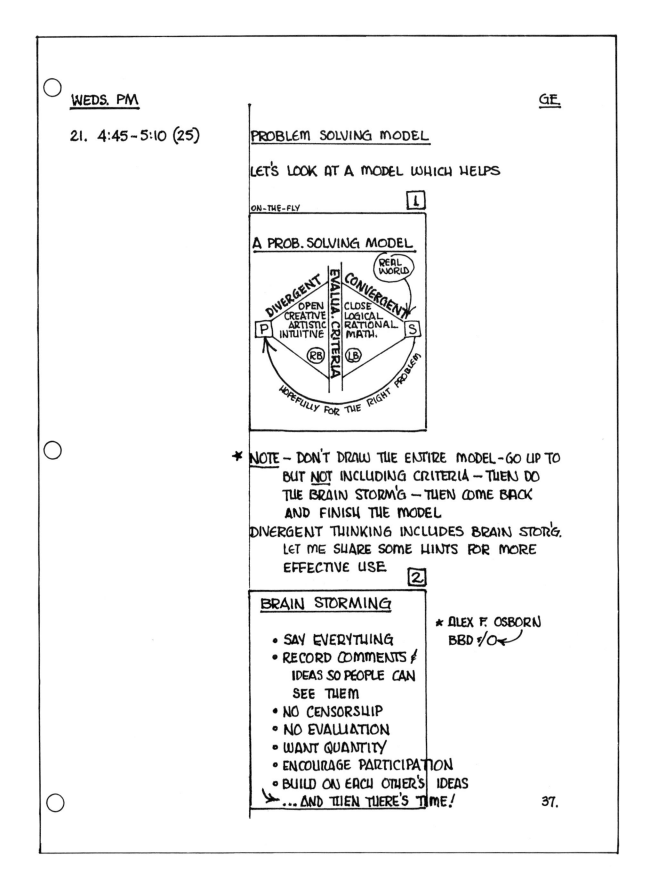

★ <u>NOTE</u> – DON'T DRAW THE ENTIRE MODEL – GO UP TO
         BUT <u>NOT</u> INCLUDING CRITERIA – THEN DO
         THE BRAIN STORM'G – THEN COME BACK
         AND FINISH THE MODEL
   DIVERGENT THINKING INCLUDES BRAIN STORG.
         LET ME SHARE SOME HINTS FOR MORE
         EFFECTIVE USE

When I use this method, sparingly, I prefer to put the tab on the preceding page instead of the chart I'm looking for. This permits me to grab the tab and flip that page, thereby revealing the one I want. Another reason I don't tab very often is that it damages the charts.

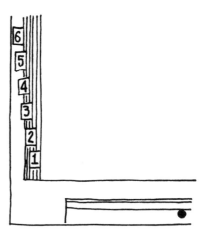

I monitored a facilitator/trainer doing a management program. The person used only one easel with predrawn charts but had all of them labeled! The thing that was interesting was that Scotch Post-It Notes™ (1½- × 2-inches) were used for tabs. They were folded in half so that the sticky part held the two halves together and to the sheet. Each tab was labeled with a felt tip pen.

In some programs you will have to refer to a previous chart. This happens regardless of the number of easels you're using. If this is a requirement, the tab is the only way to go. By the way, for easy access, this time put the tab on the chart that you want.

A third way to find your next chart is to draw arrows on the charts themselves. That means an arrow on the chart you're currently presenting to indicate where your next chart will be found. An arrow pointing to the right means go to the next easel on your right. An arrow pointing down indicates that the next chart is on the same easel. An arrow on the last easel pointing toward the right (there isn't any easel on the right) means go back to the first easel.

If you use this technique, always draw the arrows in the same place. In addition, make the arrow the same size (about three or four inches) and dark enough so you can see it from a couple of feet away. A good spot to put the arrow is the upper right corner area.

Another method of finding your charts is to *always* work your way across the two or three easels. Your first chart will be on the first easel, the second on the second easel, the third on the third easel, and then back to the first easel for your fourth chart. In this manner, you needn't refer either to your notes or to an arrow on a previous chart. The only drawback is whether or not that is a logical and impactful sequence for your presentation.

And finally (although as soon as I say that I know someone will think of a few more), standardize the position of certain repetitive charts. Some examples when using three easels:

- Objective or purpose of an exercise or unit is always on the middle or second easel.

- Process or agenda is always on the first easel.

- A summary chart is always on the middle or second easel.

"Always" is certainly a restrictive word. Even as I write this, I can think of instances where I don't "always" put the purpose of an exercise on the middle chart. Remain a little flexible, even when standardizing.

Transportation

Now, if you've done so much work on those beautiful charts, you want to move them from session to session. You don't want to do them all over every time and you want some protection for your works of art. Transportation must be considered. The charts are not of a size that is easily handled, so proper protective containers are a necessity.

There are a lot of ways to transport your charts. At one time or another, I've tried most of them. The simplest is just roll 'em up and snap a rubber band around each end. Stick it under your arm and you're all set. An extension of this creative technique is to wrap the roll in a protective sheet, tape it and write your name on it.

The preceding will work, up to a point. If you're going to ship or transport them, something else is needed. This is especially true if you fly and want to check the charts with your baggage. I'm sure some of you are thinking, *"Why in the world take a chance on the airline losing these charts after all the effort that went into them?"*

I can understand your point of view. I'm certainly aware of the risk. But for me, worse than redrawing a set of charts is carrying them. I hate to carry things from site-to-site through airports. I've shipped my tube all over the United States and a lot of the rest of the world. It's been lost twice, both times coming home from a session, and both times returned the next day.

There are a lot of ways you can transport your charts whether or not you elect to check them with your baggage. I would shy away from any carrier that is flexible enough to bend in half. A vinyl or leather bag offers very little protection.

Another way to transport your charts is with some type of folio or briefcase. There are a number of different types on the market at quite a range of prices. Perma Form has one that is made of cardboard and is pretty neat. The problem with most of these is that they just aren't the right size. As a result, the charts will slide and the edges will wrinkle or fold.

Oravisual offers two types of cases for carrying flip charts. One of them is called the Travel Case (C300) and costs about 100 dollars. It is made of fiberboard and specifically designed for the standard-size paper. The inside dimensions are a good five inches, so it'll hold plenty. The second is the Carrying Case (C301) made of reinforced leatherette. Like the Travel Case, it is designed for the standard 27- × 34-inch pads. The cost of the Carrying Case is about fifty dollars.

A variation from the industrial world is the Tube-Pak™ from Consolidated Plastics, Macedonia, Ohio (800) 321-1980. They manufacture a variety of clear plastic tubing. The tubes are sold in 8 foot sections so you'll have to cut them to size. One problem is that they're pretty expensive, and the caps to seal off the ends have to be purchased separately, in quantities of one hundred.

Some type of rigid tube is the best way to go. My colleague, Pat O'Brien, used a thick cardboard tube. I think it was the core for a large role of newsprint. Round wooden wedges were jammed in each opening. It worked well, but Pat had a heck of a time getting the wedges out.

The more flexible (it gives a little) high-impact tubes are much better. Some are manufactured specifically for transporting delicate instruments. As you might imagine, the prices vary considerably. An outstanding tube is sold by A&J Manufacturing Company in Los Angeles (800) 537-4000. A&J has one tube that is thirty inches long (remember our charts are twenty-seven inches wide) and ten inches in diameter. The 10-inch diameter reduces curling and set. To quote their brochure:

> "Made from hi-impact ABS plastic, these cases are lightweight and easy to handle. Verticle ribs are incorporated into design for extra strength.

> The bottom of the case is reinforced with a two-inch layer of polyurethane foam under a $\frac{1}{4}$-inch layer of high density polyethylene sheet. This prevents tripod tips from damaging the case and helps absorb shock during transit.

> Heavy-duty nylon strapping holds the cover securely to the tube. A heavy-duty steel spring-loaded handle is incorporated into the case for easy handling."

The case may be an outstanding one, but so's the price— about 180 dollars plus shipping charges. That's a little more than I'd care to spend.

I use a fishing rod case. I tried about three different ones until I found Rod Caddy. My Rod Caddy, Model 202A, is made of flexible high-impact plastic, with one tube fitting inside the other. You can buy it directly from the manufacturer, Bead Chain Tackle Company, for thirty-seven dollars.

The inner tube is four inches in diameter, so it holds plenty of charts. When you buy it, the inner tube, although adjustable, is about two feet longer than necessary. I suggest you cut it down so that 34¾ inches of the plastic is left. Those 34¾ inches do not include the base. Use a fine-toothed saw or take it to a plastics shop and have them cut it down. It should be cut so that the inner tube just fits in the outer one. Then drill a hole, the same size as the others you'll see, so that the edge of the hole is one-half inch from the edge (end) of the plastic. The hole is necessary in order to lock the two tubes together. The above is really not as complicated as it sounds.

The case comes with foam rubber inserts in the ends of both tubes. However, to avoid banging the ends of the charts, I recommend you buy a large bag of cotton balls. Cut the bag in half, with the balls still in it, then tape and staple each half closed and stuff one in each tube.

The tube comes in a number of different colors but I always select a bright yellow. It's very easy to see on an airport baggage carousel. My tubes last about two years. Not bad when you consider I've shipped mine around the world, and they get twice the wear and tear that a fisherman would give them in a lifetime.

I teach a one-week management seminar for new managers at General Electric's Management Institute at Crotonville, New York a couple of times a year. Because the session is a custom-designed seminar and always held at Crotonville, I leave my charts there. I don't lug them back and forth. In between my sessions, GE held a Train-the-Trainers seminar for some of their trainer/consultants. During the session, someone unrolled my flip charts to show the participants some charting examples.

When I arrived for my next session, I immediately knew that someone had unrolled my charts and used them somehow. How did I know? When the charts were re-rolled, they were rolled the wrong way. As I used them and as I taped them to the wall around the room, the charts curled up about a third of the length of the paper. They remained curled that way, on the walls, the entire week. No amount of masking tape would hold 'em down.

When you roll a set of charts, roll them under, as shown in the illustration at right. This prevents them from curling up on the easel later on. Softly drop the roll of charts into the inner tube without putting a rubber band around it. Now gently bounce the tube up and down. This will cause the roll of charts to unwind in the tube. This unwinding minimizes the set (the curl) the paper will take while stored this way.

Now you'll notice, unless you've put 150 charts in the tube, that the center provides some open space. This is where you can put your cut-off yard stick, mentioned earlier. At least a dozen markers, or more, will also fit in that space.

I can't let this section end without telling you a story of what happened one time to my charts and tube. I'd been doing a session in New Jersey. My wife and her parents, marvelous people, decided to meet me in Atlantic City when the session was over. We'd spend the weekend having some fun before my next session began on Tuesday.

Well, I did my session, met them in Atlantic City, and had a great time; even won a few bucks shootin' craps. When it came time for us to leave on Sunday evening, I gave the keys to the bell hop to get the bags from the room while I got the car. I drove up to the entrance and opened the trunk so that the bell hop could load the bags. When we arrived in Short Pump later that evening, I noticed my flip chart case was not in the trunk.

I immediately panicked and then phoned the hotel in Atlantic City. I told them about my missing charts. They called me back about 20 minutes later and had found the tube. I explained to the person I was talking to that I had a session that Tuesday in Connecticut. *"No problem,"* was the response, *"We'll mail it there for you."*

Now, there are two things I haven't mentioned. One, I had not locked this tube because I wasn't traveling by air. Second, I'd lost one of my bags of cotton balls somewhere during the session I'd just completed. So, to protect the ends of the charts, I stuffed a pair of worn underpants in one end. Well, when I arrived in Connecticut on Monday night, the tube was there waiting for me. I started to set up and opened the tube—the underwear was gone! Never did find 'em.

One last thing: when closing up the case, always slide the outer tube over the inner one. Now I know that sounds dumb; after all, the outer tube won't fit inside the inner one. Let me try to explain. Never force the inner tube down into the outer. The charts will slip out of the inner tube before it is in place. I had someone who was helping me do this and ruined an entire set of charts. The six to eight inches in the bottom were wrinkled and torn.

Storage

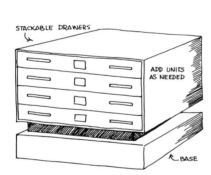

STACKABLE DRAWERS

ADD UNITS AS NEEDED

BASE

How many sets of charts do you have? I've got about twenty. Storage, therefore, is another consideration, as is identification: *"What seminar or presentation is this?"* I haven't solved this problem to my complete satisfaction. A few rolls are still lying around in corners and on top of file cabinets.

It appears that the best type of storage would be what are known as flat cabinets—the kind used in drafting and commercial art departments. Various styles and prices are available. The price will vary directly with the material (metal, plastic, or cardboard) and the size and number of drawers. The flat files have a number of advantages:

- The biggest advantage, to my mind, is that they lie flat. If you're coming off a program which required travel, with the charts in a tube, they will have a curl. You'll need to hold them down. This can be accomplished by using a piece of cardboard. The back of a flip chart pad is just the right size. A thin piece of plywood is also quite good. Incidentally, these pieces of plywood or cardboard can also be used to separate two different presentations stored in the same drawer.

- I like the fact that the drawers can be marked and thus, sets of charts are easily identifiable.

- Finally, they're out of sight. That gives me a great feeling of organization.

They do have some disadvantages:

- The sizes are not consistent with our 27- × 34-inch requirement. The best I could find is a drawer size of 30 × 42 inches. Too much room for slippin' and slidin'.

- The steel ones are expensive. For example, a five-drawer steel, 2½-inch deep flat file, 30 × 42 inches, with a stand and cap (they are stackable), is about 700 dollars.

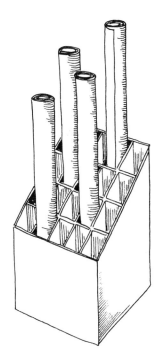

But you don't have to have steel. Many types of composition and cardboard flat files are available. One manufacturer is Perma Products Company of Dallas, Texas (214) 298-4225. Size is still a problem. You'd need one that measures 35 × 45 inches to fit the flip charts.

Perma Products, as well as a number of other companies, manufacture a variety of storage cabinets which will hold rolled charts. They have a definite advantage of requiring less space. Identification is only a bit more difficult. Finally, the cost is a lot less than the others.

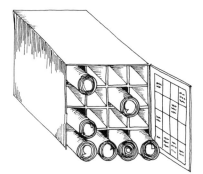

Don't worry about the rolls sticking up over the top of the storage cabinet. The key item is the size of the opening that will hold the roll. The minimum for comfort and ease is three and a half inches; four would be better. The tighter you roll them, the more curl and set you'll get on the paper. One other thing you'll have to do with these cabinets: put a rubber band around each end of the roll. If you don't so that, you'll have trouble getting the roll out or you'll pull the compartment out of the cabinet.

These cabinets are available with the roll either standing on end or lying horizontally. They vary in cost from thirty dollars for one made like a cardboard box that will hold sixteen 3-inch rolls, to 105 dollars for one with the same capacity but built of steel. Both of the above are built for 25-inch rolls so the ends will stick out. The next size is thirty-seven inches which is too long.

Of all the storage racks and cabinets available the one that comes closest to what we all need is made by Safeco Products (Minneapolis, Minnesota (612) 536-3626). They make a mobile stand (shown at the right) that will hold twelve hanging 30-inch aluminum clamps. They indicate that each clamp will hold 100

sheets. A clear plastic holder is available to identify each set. Again, the price is relatively high. The stand plus twelve clamps costs about 560 dollars.

That's what's available in the market. There are other options, some better than others. If you have the wall and the space you could do as indicated at the left. A medium binder clip on each end holds the charts together; flip one of the handles (wires) up and slip it over a nail. The charts hang, avoiding curl, and take up a minimum of room. (I did this in a closet in my old office.) The difficulty is apparent. If you want the fourth set down, you have to take the other three off—an inconvenience. Once I thought it'd be easier to undo the clip and slip the charts out. That doesn't work too well; they all fall on the floor with the resulting damage. Identification is accomplished by labeling the binder clips using correction tape and a felt pen. The problem is volume. How many sets can you hang on a nail?

Another solution is to get a carton from a hardware store or electrical contractor that is used to ship neon light bulbs. If you do this, make certain that at least six inches of the roll sticks out from the top of the box. This makes it easier to get rolls out of the box and to identify the roll itself. Of course any old cardboard will do the same thing. It's just that the light bulb boxes are longer, and the rolls won't flop around as much. Incidentally, put something heavy (a brick) in the bottom of the box.

If you're handy, you might try the rig shown on the following page. If you're not handy, you might have it made at an unpainted furniture store. This is what I built for myself and it seems to do the job. The size indicated will hold about seventeen sets depending on how you space the slots and the number of charts in each set. When the set has more charts than will fit in one clip, I split the set in two. Plans and material specifications are in Appendix A at the end of the book.

I think the thing I look for in storing my charts is ease of finding them when I need them, and a sense of organization. How that's accomplished and the sophistication of the device are a matter of personal preference.

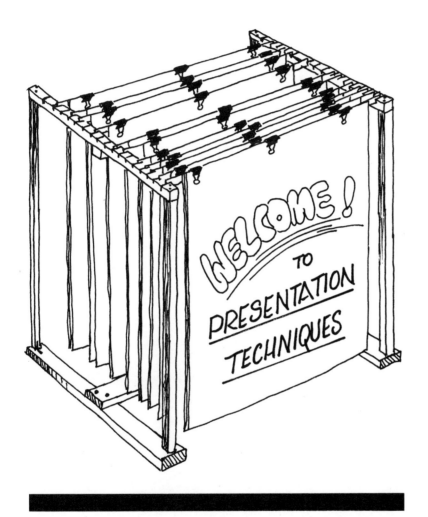

Chapter 6.

Summary

Well, I told you it wasn't a long book. I hope that somewhere in this small volume you've found some pointers that permit you to be more effective and comfortable in your next presentation. I recommend that you try some of the things we've discussed; experiment, and test them. Get some practice so you feel comfortable with whatever you're attempting, but, above all, be yourself.

Take that extra few minutes to think about your chart. Consider such items as spacing, color, and relationships. Just that few minutes alone will make a significant difference in your flip charts. Remember that good results without good planning is just good luck.

To illustrate what I've been writing about let me share another brief story with you. Bill Aboud is a friend and colleague whom I meet more in airports than anywhere else. He's a great seminar leader/instructor. His style is easy and he's extremely knowledgeable. The only criticism I've ever heard of Bill is that he can't keep his shirt tail in. Bill was on the staff of GE's Management Institute at Crotonville, New York for a number of years until he and his brother started their own consulting firm.

Bill and I did a management program at GE Crotonville some while back. It was the first time we worked together. Bill liked my chart work and said he learned a great deal from my techniques and charts. I didn't think any more about it until a mutual friend told me a little story passed on to him by Bill.

A couple of months after our session Bill was setting up his charts in preparation for the following day. The maintenance man wandered into the room and watched Bill putting the charts on the easels. After several minutes, standing there in silence, watching, he said, *"Mr. Aboud, I've known you for years and I've never seen you make such pretty charts before."* The point of the story is that these things work, they do make a difference, and your audience will notice.

Finally, if you've a question or comment that I can help with, give me a call at (804) 747-0816. If you'd like to discuss flip charts, the book, or communication techniques, let me hear from you.

Thank you for your time. Good luck on that next presentation. I know it'll be a great success. I'd also like to think I had some small measure of influence on that success.

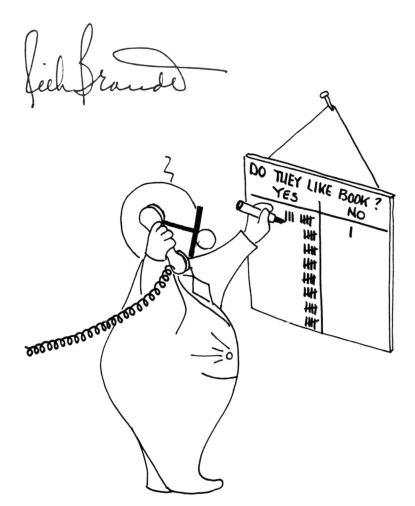

Chapter 7.

A Partial List of Resources

A&J Manufacturing Company
(Chart Tube)
P.O. Box 90596
Los Angeles, CA 90009
(800) 537-4000

American Pad & Paper Co.
(Easel Pads)
P.O. Box 1250
Holyoke, MA 01040
(413) 536-3511

Bead Chain Tackle Co.
(Rod Caddy Carrying Tube)
241 Mountain Grove St.
Bridgeport, CT 06605
(203) 334-4124

Consolidated Plastics Co.
(Plastic Tubes)
1864 Enterprise Pkwy.
Twinsburg, OH 44087
(800) 321-1980

Da-Lite Screen Co., Inc.
*(Oravisual Products:
Easels, Paper, Cases)*
P.O. Box 137
Warsaw, IN 46580
(219) 267-8101

Fidelity Products Co.
(Storage Cabinets & Supplies)
P.O. Box 155
Minneapolis, MN 55440
(800) 328-3034

Gillette Company
(El Marko Markers)
Prudential Center
Boston, MA 02199
(617) 421-7000

Griffin Manufacturing Co.
(Yardstick Compass)
P.O. Box 308
Webster, NY 14580
(716) 265-1991

Keuffel & Esser Co.
(Leroy Lettering Sets)
20 Whippany Rd.
Morristown, NJ 07960
(201) 285-5000

Kroy Industries, Inc.
(Lettering Device)
Graphics Division
1728 Gervais Avenue
St. Paul, MN 55109
(612) 770-7000

Memindex
(Storage Boxes)
149 Carter Street
Rochester, NY 14601
(716) 342-7740

Perma Products Co.
(Storage Cabinets)
P.O. Box 24728
Dallas, TX 75224
(800) 527-3198

Safeco Products Co.
(Hanging Chart Stand)
9300 Research Ctr. Rd. W.
Minneapolis, MN 55428
(612) 536-6700

The Screen Works, Inc.
(Easels)
3925 N. Pulaski
Chicago, IL 60641
(312) 588-8380

Stikky Wax Corp.
3721 N. Broadway
Chicago, IL 60612
(312) 528-8860

Viking Office Products
(Markers & Tape)
4630 Interstate Drive
Cincinnati, OH 45426
(800) 421-1222

Welsh Sporting Goods
(Individual Supplies Kit)
Boyt Division
P.O. Box 220
Iowa Falls, IA 50126
(515) 648-4626

Appendix A.

Flip Chart Stand

Materials Required:

Item	Qty.	Description	Est. Cost
1.	1	2″ × 4″ × 8′ wood	$ 1.79
2.	1	2″ × 2″ × 8′ wood	1.59
3.	2	2″ × 2″ × 6′ wood	2.40
4.	8	1-1/2″ corner braces with screws	3.18
5.	6	1/8″ × 3/4″ × 8′ aluminum bars	23.70
6.	24	2″ No. 12, flat head wood screws	2.70
7.	54	IDL medium, No. 5, binder clips	7.43
		Total Estimated Cost	**$42.79**

Construction Steps:

1. Cut all lumber to size. Use the drawing on the following page which references the piece identification, letters, together with the instructions below:

   - Using Item 1 (2″ × 4″ × 8′) cut two (2) "C" pieces, each 24 inches long and one (1) "D" piece, 33 inches long.

   - Using Item 2 (2″ × 4″ × 8′) cut two (2) "A" pieces, each 24 inches long and one (1) "E" piece, 31 inches long.

   - Using Item 3 (2″ × 2″ × 6′) cut four (4) "B" pieces, each 34 inches long. You'll actually cut two (2) pieces from each board.

2. Drill holes for the 2-inch screws using a 7/32 drill bit. A 15/64 will also work and make the job a bit easier, however, the screw will not take as much of a bite as the 7/32 hole.

3. Using a countersink bit, enlarge the top part of the holes you've just drilled so that the heads of the 2-inch screws will be recessed below the surface of the wood.

4. Cut slots in the two "A" pieces, from Step 1 above, for the aluminum strips. The slots are 1/2 inch deep and 3/16 inch wide. Remember the aluminum bar is 1/8 inch thick. The bar has to fit in the slots. Your first cut is made 1 1/2 inches from the end of piece "A," after which the cuts are spaced

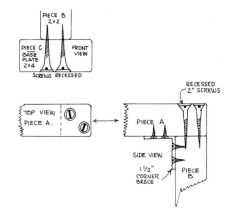

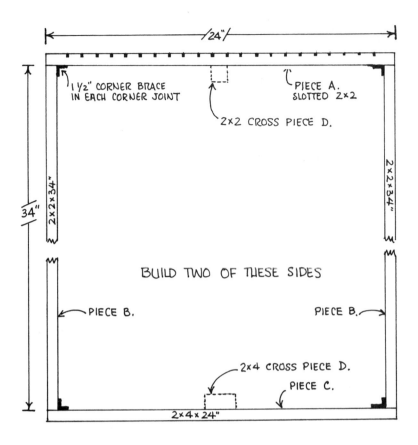

BUILD TWO OF THESE SIDES

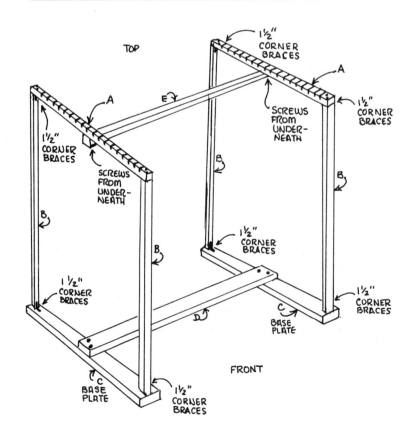

Appendix A: **Flip Chart Stand**

1¼ inches apart. This will give you seventeen slots, sixteen of which are usable. One of them will be well over the top cross piece "E."

I spaced the slots 1¼ inches apart on my stand but in looking at it I believe that you could space them one inch apart without any problem. If you don't need the extra four slots I would recommend making the slots 1¼ inches apart for easier removal and insertion of the chart sets.

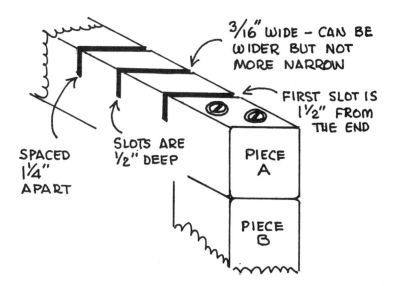

5. Assemble two sides as shown in the drawing. The four corners are held by two two-inch flat head scews and a 1½-inch corner brace at each joint. The tops of the flat head screws should be recessed.

6. Connect the two sides by first screwing down piece "D," the bottom crosspiece. The ends of "D" are flush with the outside edge of "C." Then turn the whole thing upside down and screw on piece "E," the 2- × 2-inch upper cross piece.

   At first, I thought that I would need a diagonal board or some type of turnbuckle to keep the stand steady. But, I found that the stand is rigid and doesn't wobble. If yours wobbles for some reason you may want to add a diagonal brace of some kind. However, if your cuts are square and the correct length, I don't think you'll need it.

7. Cut each 8-foot aluminum bar into 31-inch sections using a fine-toothed hacksaw. Incidentally, six aluminum bars will give you eighteen strips. If you went for the one-inch spacing you'll need another bar. The same thing is true of the number of clips. Fifty-four clips are necessary for eighteen strips. You'll note that the ends of the bar, after

sawing, have sharp edges and perhaps a few burrs. Use a fine-toothed file to smooth and slightly round these edges. That may save you from a nasty cut later on.

Now you're ready to store your charts! Use three binder clips on each set. Straighten out your charts. (I find this can only be done on the floor.) Line up the top of the charts with the edge of one of the aluminum strips. Now clip strip and charts together with one of the binder clips. Work your way across the strip—start at one end, then the middle, and finally the other end. If you clip both ends first you'll probably have a bulge in the middle which causes some difficulty smoothing out the charts. If the tops are uneven or corners lost or damaged, turn the set over and clip it from the bottom of the charts. Identify the set by sticking a label (correction tape) on one of the binder clips and you're all set.

Feels good to be organized doesn't it?

Appendix B.

Templates

Thumbs-Up Template

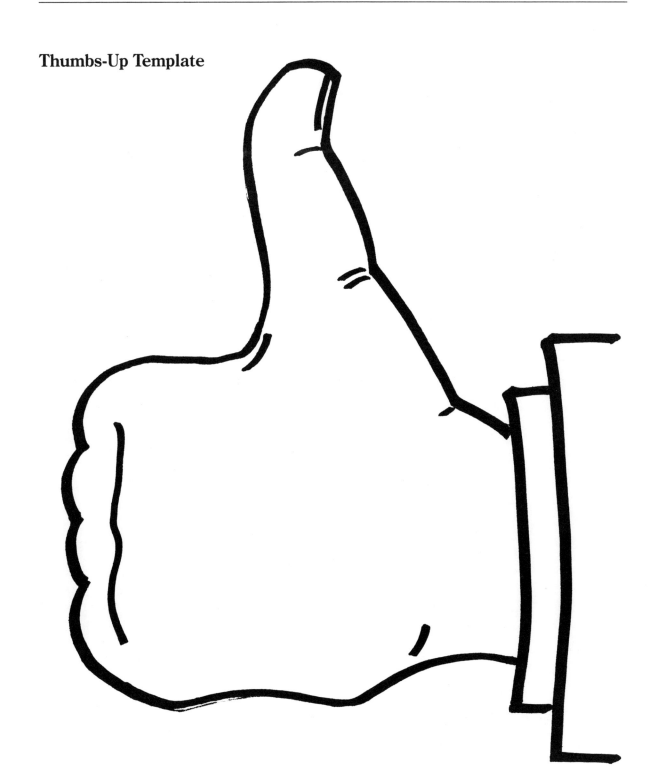

Cuckoo Clock Template

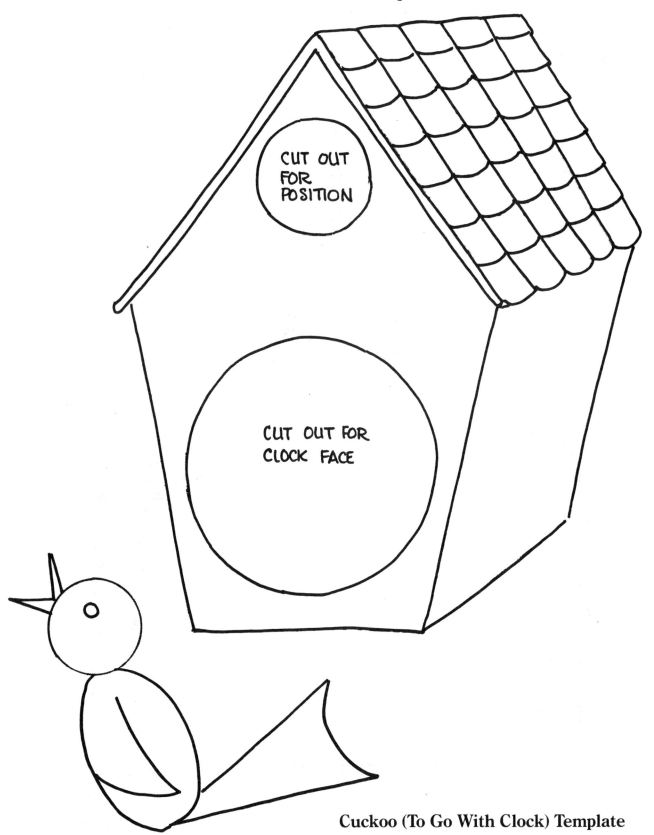

CUT OUT
FOR
POSITION

CUT OUT FOR
CLOCK FACE

Cuckoo (To Go With Clock) Template

About Richard C. Brandt

Richard C. Brandt served as president and principal consultant/trainer of Brandt Management Group, Inc. (BMG) of Richmond, Virginia. Brandt Management Group has built a quality reputation with its clients, which include CitiCorp, I.E. DuPont de Nemours, Goodyear Tire and Rubber, Monsanto, Chase Manhatten Bank, and other top names in American business and industry. In addition to BMG's work in presentation techniques, it has received critical acclaim for its two-day workshop/seminar "The Business of Listening." The program features the unique Listening Practices Feedback Report. The research-based computerized report is now being used in a variety of client programs, for example, sales, communications, and management.

Rich brought to his consulting and training activities over thirty years of business experience, most of it at the managerial and executive levels. He was associated with Reynolds Metals Company and its affiliate, Robertshaw Controls, The Computer Company, and Blue Cross of Virginia before organizing BMG in 1978. As a result, he related very well to the "real world." This permitted him a level of examples and vignettes not enjoyed by some other trainers and consultants. His work was light, characterized by humor and practical comments and only slightly marred by theory and academia, and he was a much sought-after speaker.

He received an undergraduate degree in management from St. John's University and an MBA from NYU's Graduate School of Business Administration. He also received additional training from various organizations: IBM's Executive Institute in San Jose, California, The Creative Problem Solving Institute at the State University College at Buffalo, and University Associates.

Rich and his wife, Jan, had four children, all of whom became successful. Jan worked with her husband, specializing in group dynamics, listening, and creativity. Rich was an avid fisherman and held the Virginia Anglers Club record for Largemouth Bass. He also designed, painted, and collected military miniatures, more commonly known as toy soldiers. His interest in this area was focused on the Napoleonic era.

*Lives of great men
all remind us
We can make our
lives sublime,
And, departing,
leave behind us
Footprints on the
sands of time.*

—From A Psalm of Life
*Henry Wadsworth
Longfellow*

Index

Selected Illustrations